LET'S FIND OUT!

INDIA'S SPACE ADVENTURE

Biman Basu

RED PANDA

RED PANDA

First published by Red Panda, an imprint of Westland Publications Limited, in 2020

Published by Red Panda, an imprint of Westland Books, a division of Nasadiya Technologies Private Limited, in 2023

No. 269/2B, First Floor, 'Irai Arul', Vimalraj Street, Nethaji Nagar, Alapakkam Main Road, Maduravoyal, Chennai 600095

Westland, the Westland logo, Red Panda and the Red Panda logo are the trademarks of Nasadiya Technologies Private Limited, or its affiliates.

Images sourced with permission from ISRO and NASA

ISBN: 9789395767446
10 9 8 7 6 5 4 3

Book design by New Media Line Creations, New Delhi

Printed at Parksons Graphics Pvt. Ltd

LET'S FIND OUT!

INDIA'S SPACE ADVENTURE

BIMAN BASU

RED PANDA

The red panda is a reddish-brown mammal with a long, ringed tail and a raccoon-like face. Also called firefox, it is found in the forests of the eastern Himalayas. In India, it lives in Sikkim, Arunachal Pradesh, Darjeeling district in West Bengal and parts of Meghalaya. Its diet includes bamboo shoots and leaves, grass, fruit, roots and insects. The cat-sized red panda uses its bushy tail for balance and to wrap around its body for warmth up in the mountains.

The red panda is now an endangered species, with less than 10,000 left in the wild.

CONTENTS

WHAT IS SPACE?

Space begins where the Earth's atmosphere ends. No one knows exactly how vast space is but we know that travelling at 3,00,000 km per second, light takes billions of years to reach the Earth from some distant stars and galaxies. Astronomers measure distances in space, not in metres or kilometres, but in light-years, the distance light travels in one year (roughly 9.3 trillion km).

The Earth is surrounded by an envelope of air that we call the atmosphere. It consists of a mixture of gases—mainly nitrogen, oxygen, carbon dioxide, water vapour and minute amounts of other gases. The Earth's atmosphere is most dense near the ground and becomes thinner as we go up. Weather phenomena, such as storms and rain, happen only within the atmosphere.

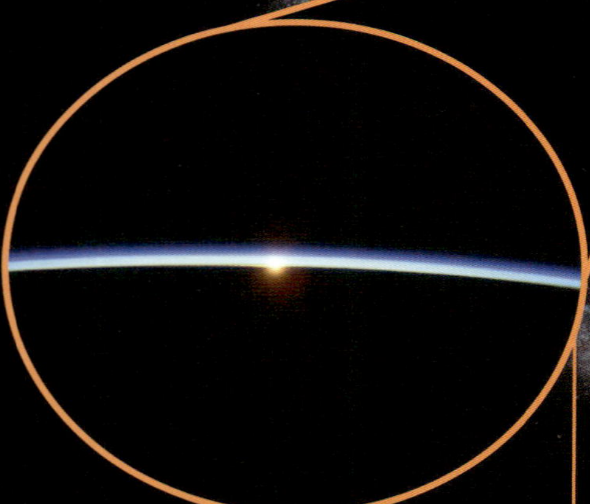

Beyond 100 km from the ground, the atmosphere is extremely thin, like a vacuum. The imaginary boundary that starts at this point has been named the Karman Line.

Stars, planets, our solar system, galaxies, the Milky Way—all exist in space. Stars are giant balls of fire that emit their own light and radiate heat, like the Sun. All stars, except our Sun, appear as points of light because of their distance from the Earth. Similar to our solar system, most stars have their own planetary systems. Planets are small bodies that orbit their central stars. They do not emit light and are visible only by the reflected light of their parent stars.

A galaxy is a huge collection of gas, dust and billions of stars and their planetary systems. It is held together by gravity. Our galaxy, the Milky Way, contains an estimated 25 billion to 40 billion stars and stretches across some 1,05,700 light-years.

In absence of the atmosphere, sound cannot travel in space. However, astronauts use radios to stay in communication while in space, since radio waves can still be sent and received.

Space is a mysterious and largely unexplored place. It is dark, extremely cold and has a temperature that is less than −270.45°C. It is also exposed to lethal radiations. Humans cannot go to space without adequate protection. They have to wear special spacesuits and carry oxygen with them.

WHY WE GO TO SPACE

The objective of space travel is to explore the solar system and expand our knowledge about the universe. As a result, human beings have been studying the planets in the solar system, asteroids and other space objects. The number of satellites in the Earth's orbit is also growing, offering numerous benefits, such as Earth observation, long-distance communication and navigation.

In 1865, Jules Verne published his novel about space travel, *From the Earth to the Moon*. The real space age, however, began almost a century later on 4 October 1957, with the launch of the first artificial satellite *Sputnik-1* by the former Soviet Union (now Russia). Since then, many other countries, including India, have launched their own space programmes.

Spacecraft are launched into space, from where they send back thousands of stunning photos and reveal previously unknown details about the planets. They also send back a wealth of data with exciting facts. These crewless, robotic spacecraft are called space probes.

So far, 12 astronauts have successfully landed on the Moon and returned safely to the Earth. They have brought back samples of lunar rock, which gave scientists new clues about the formation of the Moon.

The space probes *Messenger*, *Magellan*, *Juno* and *New Horizons*, have sent back new views of Mercury, Venus, Jupiter and Pluto, which has changed our perception of these members of our solar system.

Both China and the US have landed new space probes on Mars and the Moon. In 2018, the NASA space probe *InSight* landed on Mars and became the first mission designed to study the deep interiors of the planet. China's *Chang'e 4* lunar exploration mission accomplished the first soft landing on the far side of the Moon in 2019. And NASA launched *Lucy*, in 2021, the first mission to explore the Jupiter Trojan asteroids that share the orbit of Jupiter around the Sun. *Lucy* was able to capture views of four Jupiter Trojan asteroids, in February 2023.

HOW TO GO TO SPACE

It is possible to travel in the air from one place to another, on Earth, because the atmosphere is thick enough to support the flying of aircraft. Besides, the oxygen present in the atmosphere allows the burning of air fuel, which powers aircraft engines. In the vacuum of space, however, rockets are the only mode of transport.

SPACE: A 3-IN-1 PROGRAMME

A space programme has three components:

- A satellite that is placed in an orbit
- A rocket that is powerful enough to launch the satellite in the desired orbit
- A system of ground stations to send and receive signals to and from the satellite

In most countries, space programmes are limited to launching spacecraft and satellites for different purposes, such as telecommunications, remote sensing, weather observation, and TV and radio broadcasting. After the launch, satellites usually remain in their assigned orbits to carry out their tasks. For missions to the Moon and various planets, spacecraft are steered into specific paths towards their destinations, using onboard rockets.

SATELLITES

Satellites are used for various purposes, such as long-distance telecommunication, television networking, weather observation and solar-system exploration.

Navigation satellites provide positioning, navigation and timing services, globally and regionally. One of the primary services offered by the Global Navigation Satellite System (GNSS) is GPS (Global Positioning System).

A communication satellite is placed in a circular orbit around the earth. The satellite moves in the direction of the Earth's rotation with the same speed, so it appears stationary to us. This is why the orbit is called the geostationary orbit.

Remote-sensing satellites or Earth-observation satellites are special satellites designed to study the Earth's surface from a height of 500–600 km. These are usually placed in a north-south oriented polar orbit, passing over both the poles, to help cover the entire Earth in a span of 16 to 22 days.

Some of the newest satellites to be launched by ISRO, in 2023, include *NVS-01*, the first of the second-generation satellites meant for the Navigation with Indian Constellation (*NavIC*), *EOS-07* and *AzaadiSAT-2*, a combined effort of 750 Indian girl students.

ROCKETS

Satellites have no use until they are placed in their intended orbits. They are launched from the Earth via large cylindrical vehicles called rockets that carry satellites and humans into space.

Space rockets work on the same principle as the small rocket used during Diwali, i.e., they move by forcing out burning gases from the bottom. Diwali rockets use a powder mixture packed in a paper cylinder. When the wick at the bottom is lit, the powder starts burning, and the gases produced escape from below at high speed, pushing the rocket up.

Since there is no oxygen in space, rockets must carry their own oxygen in the form of chemicals called oxidisers along with the fuel. When rocket fuel is ignited, it combines with the oxidiser, producing huge amounts of gases that are ejected forcefully. A rocket is propelled by the release of hot gases coming out of its bottom end with a lot of force—a principle known as Newton's Third Law of Motion, which states that for every action, there is an equal and opposite reaction.

Rockets are made of several 'stages' that fall away one by one, after the launch. This allows rockets to reach very high speeds. Rocket stages use different kinds of propellants—solid, liquid, or even liquid gases (such as hydrogen and oxygen) stored at extremely low temperatures (below –220°C). The third kind is called the cryogenic stage.

Rockets can be of many types. Small rockets or sounding rockets are used for probing and space research. They are single- or two-stage and use solid propellants. Rockets for launching satellites are made up of at least three or four stages and have an upper cryogenic stage.

GROUND-CONTROL STATIONS

All satellites in orbit are guided and controlled from the ground through radio signals. When a satellite is placed in a low-Earth orbit, it needs to be monitored using a turning dish antenna to maintain radio contact.

A satellite ground-control station continually receives data from a satellite regarding its position. In case of any deviation, small thrusters onboard are fired to correct the deviation. The ground-control also maintains the proper orientation of the solar panels on the satellite for optimum power generation.

In India, the ISRO Telemetry, Tracking and Command Network (ISTRAC) at Bengaluru monitors satellites in low-Earth orbit, such as *Aryabhata*, *Bhaskara* and *Rohini*. The network functions through ground stations at Bengaluru, Lucknow, Port Blair, Sriharikota, Thiruvananthapuram, Bears Lake in Russia, and Mauritius.

Space Shuttle: The Reusable Spacecraft

NASA's Space Shuttle was the world's first reusable spacecraft. It took off like a rocket and landed on a runway like a glider. It could be used repeatedly, and was designed to carry astronauts and large payloads, such as satellites, into orbit and back. The reusability of the Space Shuttle substantially reduced the cost of human space missions. In all, six space shuttles were built, which together made a total of 135 flights. They are *Enterprise*, *Columbia*, *Challenger*, *Discovery*, *Atlantis* and *Endeavour*.

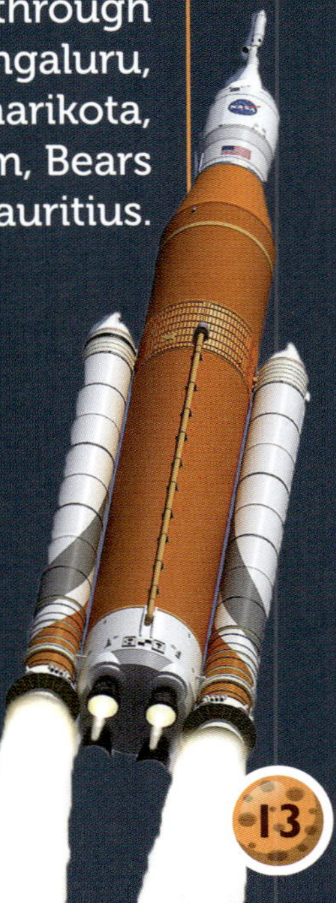

WORKING IN SPACE

Astronauts who travel to space stay in space stations.

A space station is a large spacecraft where a human crew can live and work for long periods. It provides a unique environment for scientists to carry out experiments in the absence of gravity, which cannot be done on Earth. Astronauts are given rigorous training on working in zero-gravity condition, often on parabolic flights, which simulate the sensation of free fall.

The absence of gravity in a space station affects astronauts in many ways. It can weaken their muscles and bones and cause disorientation. Weightlessness also makes many simple operations challenging. To avoid these problems, astronauts have to follow a special regimen of physical exercises.

The world's first space station, *Salyut 1*, was launched by the former Soviet Union in 1971.

In 1984, Indian Air Force pilot Squadron Leader Rakesh Sharma became the first Indian citizen to travel in space. He flew aboard *Soyuz T-11* to the *Salyut 7* space station. He spent seven days, 21 hours and 40 minutes aboard *Salyut 7*. During this time, his team conducted scientific and technical studies, including 43 experimental sessions, mainly in the fields of biomedicine and remote sensing.

The International Space Station (ISS) is the largest and longest operating space station till date. It is a joint project between five participating space agencies—NASA, Roscosmos, Japan Aerospace Exploration Agency (JAXA), European Space Agency (ESA) and Canadian Space Agency (CSA). It was built in orbit over many years, beginning in 1998.

Today, the ISS is the largest human-made object to have ever been put in orbit. It serves as a research laboratory for conducting a wide range of experiments in zero gravity. The station is also ideal for testing the spacecraft systems and equipment required for missions to the Moon and Mars.

1962 *to* 1991

1962
- Indian National Committee for Space Research (INCOSPAR) formed by the Department of Atomic Energy
- Work on establishing Thumba Equatorial Rocket Launching Station (TERLS) started

1963
- First sounding rocket launched from TERLS (21 November)

1965
- Space Science & Technology Centre (SSTC) found in Thumba

1969
- Indian Space Research Organisation (ISRO) was formed under the Department of Atomic Energy (15 August)

1972
- Space Commission and Department of Space set up (1 June)
- ISRO brought under DOS

1975
- First Indian Satellite, *Aryabhata*, launched from the former Soviet Union (19 April)

1975-76
- Satellite Instructional Television Experiment (SITE) conducted with American *ATS-6* satellite

1977
- Satellite Telecommunication Experiments Project (STEP) carried out with Franco-German *Symphonie* satellite

1979
- *Bhaskara-I* launched from former Soviet Union (7 June)
- First experimental launch of *SLV-3* with *Rohini* satellite onboard from SDSC, Sriharikota, but satellite not placed in orbit (10 August)

1980
- Second Experimental launch of *SLV-3* from SDSC, Sriharikota and *Rohini* satellite placed in orbit (18 July)

1981
- *APPLE* launched from Kourou, French Guiana (19 June)
- *Bhaskara-II* launched from the former Soviet Union (20 November)

1982

62 YEARS of Space Missions

- *INSAT-1A* launched from the USA (10 April)

983

- *NSAT-1B* aunched from he USA 30 August)

1984

- The first Indian, Squadron Leader Rakesh Sharma, sent to space as part of an Indo-Soviet manned space mission (April)

1987

- First developmental launch of *ASLV* with *SROSS-1* satellite onboard (24 March) from SHAR but satellite not placed in orbit

1988

- Launch of first operational Indian remote-sensing satellite, *IRS-1A* from the former Soviet Union (17 March)
- *INSAT-1C* launched from USA (21 July)

1990

- *INSAT-1D* launched from the USA (12 June)

1991

- Second operational remote-sensing satellite, *IRS-1B*, launched from the former Soviet Union (29 August)

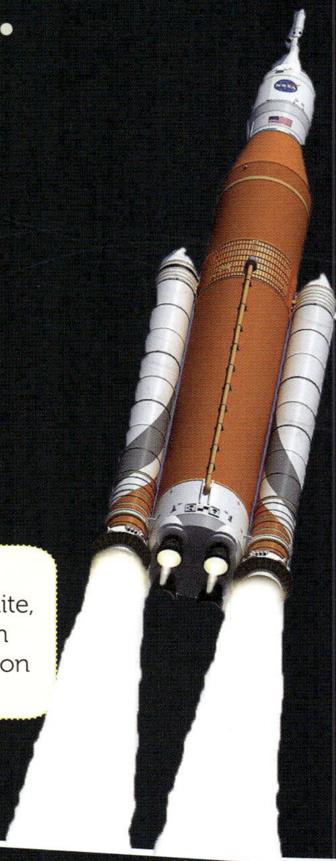

1992 *to* 2011

1992

- *INSAT-2A*, the first satellite of the indigenously built second-generation INSAT series, launched from Kourou, French Guiana (10 July)

1993

- *INSAT-2B*, the second satellite in the *INSAT-2* series, launched from Kourou, French Guiana (23 July)
- First developmental launch of *PSLV* with *IRS-1E* onboard (20 September) from SHAR but satellite not placed in orbit

1994

- Fourth developmental launch of *ASLV* with *SROSS-C2* onboard from SHAR and satellite placed in orbit (4 May)

1995

- *INSAT-2C*, the third satellite in the *INSAT-2* series, launched from Kourou, French Guiana (7 December)
- *IRS-1C* launched from the former Soviet Union (28 December)

1996

- Third developmental launch of *PSLV* with *IRS-P3* onboard from SHAR and satellite placed in polar Sun-synchronous orbit (21 March)

1997

- *INSAT-2D*, fourth satellite in the *INSAT-2* series, launched from Kourou, French Guiana (4 June)
- First operational launch of *PSLV* with *IRS-1D* onboard from SHAR and satellite placed in orbit (29 September)

1999

- *INSAT-2E*, the last satellite in the multipurpose *INSAT-2* series, launched from Kourou, French Guiana (3 April)
- Indian remote-sensing satellite, *IRS-P4 (OCEANSAT)*, along with Korean *KITSAT-3* and German *DLR-TUBSAT* by *PSLV-C2* launched from SHAR (26 May)

2000

- *INSAT-3B*, the first satellite in the third generation *INSAT-3* series, launched from Kourou, French Guiana (22 March)

2001

- The first developmental launch of *GSLV-D1* with *GSAT-1* onboard from SHAR. Placed the satellite in a lower orbit (18 April)
- Launch of three satellites—*Technology Experiment Satellite* (*TES*) of ISRO, *BIRD* of Germany and *PROBA* of Belgium—by *PSLV-C3* into their intended orbits from SHAR (22 October)

2002

- India's multipurpose satellite *INSAT-3C* launched from Kourou, French Guiana (24 January)
- India's first dedicated meteorological satellite, *KALPANA-1*, launched by *PSLV-C4* from SDSC (12 September)

2003

- *INSAT-3A* launched from Kourou, French Guiana (10 April)
- India's communication satellite *INSAT-3E* launched from Kourou, French Guiana (28 September)
- Advanced remote-sensing satellite *RESOURCESAT-1 (IRS-P6)* launched by *PSLV-C5* from SDSC (17 October)

2004

- The first operational flight of *GSLV* (*GSLV-F01*) launched *EDUSAT* from SDSC (20 September)

2005

- *CARTOSAT-1* and *HAMSAT* satellites launched by *PSLV-C6* from SDSC (5 May)
- The first *INSAT* satellite, *INSAT-4A* launched from Kourou, French Guiana (22 December)

2006

- The second operational flight of *GSLV* (*GSLV-F02*) unsuccessful, and both the rocket and the communications satellite *INSAT-4C* destroyed over the Bay of Bengal (10 July)

2007

- *CARTOSAT-2,* Space Capsule Recovery Experiment (*SRE-1*), launched using *PSLV-C7* from SDSC (10 January)
- Indian communication satellite *INSAT-4B* launched from Kourou, French Guiana (12 March)
- Italian astronomical satellite *AGILE* launched by *PSLV-C8* from SDSC (April 23)
- Communication satellite *INSAT-4CR* launched by *GSLV-F04* from SDSC (2 September)

2008

- Israeli reconnaissance satellite *TECSAR* launched by *PSLV-C10* from SDSC (21 January)
- 10 satellites including India's *CARTOSAT-2A* launched by *PSLV-C9* from SDSC (28 April)
- *Chandrayaan-1,* India's first Moon Mission launched by *PSLV-C11* from SDSC (22 October)
- *Moon Impact Probe* released from *Chandrayaan-1,* crashes on the lunar surface with the Indian tricolour (14 November)

2009

- *RISAT-2* and *ANUSAT* launched by *PSLV-C12* from SDSC (20 April)
- Seven satellites—*OCEANSAT-2*, four *CUBESAT* satellites and two *RUBIN-9* satellites—launched by *PSLV-C14* from SDSC (23 September)

2010

- *GSLV-D3* carrying communication satellite *GSAT-4* satellite launched from SDSC but satellite not placed in orbit (15 April)
- Five satellites launched by *PSLV-C15* from SDSC (12 July)

2011

- Three satellites—*RESOURCESAT-2, YOUTHSAT* and *X-SAT*—launched by *PSLV-C16* from SDSC (20 April)
- Communication satellite *GSAT-8* launched by *Ariane-5* launch vehicle from Kourou, French Guiana (21 May)
- Communication satellite *GSAT-12* launched by *PSLV-C17* from SDSC (15 July)
- Weather satellite *Megha-Tropiques, CUBESAT* satellites *Jugnu* and *VESSELSAT-1,* and nanosatellite *SRMSat* launched by *PSLV-C18* from SDSC (12 October)

2012 *to* 2024

2012

- Radar imaging satellite *RISAT-1* launched by *PSLV-C19* from SDSC (26 April)
- French Earth observation satellite *SPOT 6* and Japanese microsatellite *PROITERES* launched by *PSLV-C21* from SDSC (9 September)
- Communication satellite *GSAT-10* launched from Kourou, French Guiana (29 September)

2013

- Indo-French satellite *SARAL* and six commercial payloads launched by *PSLV-C20* from SDSC (25 February)
- *IRNSS-1A*, the first satellite of India's own satellite navigation system NavIC, launched by *PSLV-C22* from SDSC (1 July)
- Indian meteorological, data relay and satellite-aided search and rescue satellite *INSAT-3D* launched from Kourou, French Guiana (26 July)
- India's multi-band military communications satellite *GSAT-7* or *INSAT-4F* launched from Kourou, French Guiana (30 August)
- *Mars Orbiter Mission* spacecraft or *Mangalyaan* launched by *PSLV-C25* from SDSC (5 November)

2014

- Communication satellite *GSAT-14* launched by *GSLV-D5* from SDSC (5 January)
- *IRNSS-1B*, the second satellite of India's own satellite navigation system NavIC, launched by *PSLV-C24* from SDSC (4 April)
- French Earth observation satellite *SPOT-7* and four co-passenger satellites launched by *PSLV-C23* from SDSC (30 June)
- *IRNSS-1C*, the third satellite of India's own satellite navigation system NavIC, launched by *PSLV-C26* from SDSC (16 October)
- Indian advanced communication satellite *GSAT-16* launched from Kourou, French Guiana (7 December)

2015

- *IRNSS-1D*, the fourth satellite of India's own satellite navigation system NavIC, launched by *PSLV-C27* from SDSC (28 March)
- Three identical *DMC-3* high-resolution optical Earth-imaging satellites and two auxiliary satellites from the UK launched by *PSLV-C28* (10 July)
- Geostationary communication satellite *GSAT-6* launched by *GSLV-D6* from SDSC (27 August)
- India's first dedicated multi-wavelength space telescope *ASTROSAT* and six satellites from international customers launched by *PSLV-C30* (28 September)
- Indian communication satellite *GSAT-15* launched from Kourou, French Guiana (11 November)
- Six satellites of Singapore launched by *PSLV-C29* from SDSC (16 December)

2016

- *IRNSS-1G*, the seventh satellite of India's own satellite navigation system NavIC, launched by *PSLV-C33* from SDSC (28 April)
- Reusable Launch Vehicle-Technology Demonstrator (RLV-TD) flight tested from SDSC (23 May)
- *CARTOSAT-2* series satellite for Earth observation together with 19 co-passenger satellites from four countries launched by *PSLV-C34* from SDSC (22 June)
- *INSAT-3DR*, an advanced weather satellite, launched by *GSLV-F05* from SDSC (8 September)
- *SCATSAT-1*, a satellite for weather-related studies, and seven co-passenger satellites from three countries launched by *PSLV-C35* from SDSC (26 September)
- Indian communication satellite *GSAT-18* launched from Kourou, French Guiana (6 October)
- Remote-sensing satellite *RESOURCESAT-2A* launched by *PSLV-C36* from SDSC (7 December)

... THE JOURNEY Continues ...

2017

- *CARTOSAT-2* series satellite for Earth observation and 103 co-passenger satellites by *PSLV-C37* launched from SDSC, setting a record (15 February)
- *GSAT-9*, also known as *South Asia Satellite*, launched by *GSLV-F09* from SDSC (5 May)
- Indian communication satellite *GSAT-19* launched by *GSLV Mk-III-D1* from SDSC (5 June)
- *CARTOSAT-2* series satellite for Earth observation and 30 co-passenger satellites launched by *PSLV-C38* from SDSC (23 June)
- India's communication satellite *GSAT-17* launched from Kourou, French Guiana (29 June)

2018

- *CARTOSAT-2* series satellite for Earth observation along with 30 co-passenger satellites launched by *PSLV-C40* from SDSC (12 January)
- Communication satellite *GSAT-6A* launched by *GSLV-F08* from SDSC (29 March)
- *IRNSS-1I*, the eighth satellite of India's own satellite navigation system NavIC, launched *PSLV-C41* from SDSC (12 April)
- Two foreign Earth-observation satellites *NovaSAR* and *S1-4* launched by *PSLV-C42* from SDSC (16 September)
- *GSAT-29*, a high-throughput communication satellite, launched by *GSLV Mk-III-D2* from SDSC (14 November)
- India's high-throughput communication satellite, *GSAT-11*, launched from Kourou, French Guiana (5 December)
- Communication satellite *GSAT-7A* launched by *GSLV-F11* from SDSC (19 December)

2019

- Military-imaging satellite *Microsat-R* and *Kalamsat-V2*, a student payload satellite, successfully injected into two different orbits by *PSLV-C44* (24 January)
- India's first electronic surveillance satellite, *EMISAT*, and 28 international customer satellites successfully injected into their designated orbits by *PSLV-C45* (1 April)
- Radar-imaging Earth-observation satellite *RISAT-2B* launched by *PSLV-C46* from SDSC (22 May)
- *Chandrayaan-2* spacecraft launched by *GSLV Mk-III-M1* from SDSC (22 July)
- *CARTOSAT-3* launched by *PSLV-C47* from SDSC (27 November)
- Twelve IAF pilots selected as potential astronauts for the *Gaganyaan* project
- Indian radar-imaging Earth-observation satellite *RISAT-2BR1* launched from SDSC by *PSLV-C48* (December 11)

2020

- Telecommunication satellite *GSAT-30* launched successfully from Kourou launch base in French Guiana by *Ariane-5* (17 January)
- PSLV successfully launched *EOS-01* and nine customer satellite from Sriharikota. (7 November)
- Communication satellite *CMS-01* launched by *PSLV-C50* (17 December 17)

2021

- Earth observation satellite *Amazonia-1* and 18 co-passenger satellites were launched to monitor deforestation in the Amazon region (February 28)

2022

- *PSLV-C54* successfully launched *EOS-06* satellite along with 8 nano-satellites (26 November)
- *LVM3 M2/OneWeb India-1 Mission* successfully placed 36 satellites into their intended orbits (October 23)
- India's Polar Satellite Launch Vehicle *PSLV-C52* injected Earth Observation Satellite *EOS-04* (14 February)

2023

- India launched the *Chandratyaan* 3 moon mission with a moon lander and rover on board the *LVM3*, Launch Vehicle Mark-3 (July 14)
- *GSLV-F12/NVS-01* mission deployed *NVS-01* navigation satellite into a Geosynchronous Transfer Orbit (May 22)
- ISRO successfully conducted the Reusable Launch Vehicle Autonomous Landing Mission (RLV LEX) at Chitradurga, Karnataka (April 2)
- The second developmental flight of Small Satellite Launch Vehicle (SSLV), *SSLV-D2* was successfully launched from the first launch pad at Sriharikota (February 10)
- PSLV-C57 successfully launched *Aditya-L1* spacecraft, the first Indian space based observatory to study the Sun from a halo orbit around first Sun-Earth Lagrangian point (L1) (September 2)

2024

- India's maiden solar mission *Aditya-L1* reached the L1 point 127 days after it was launched (January 6)

India launched its first rocket—the *Nike-Apache*, on 21 November 1963.

The launching pad was built in Thumba, a small fishing village near Thiruvananthapuram in Kerala. Thumba was chosen because it is located close to the magnetic equator of the Earth, making it an ideal site for conducting studies of the upper atmosphere and the ionosphere using rockets.

At Thumba, the first office of the Indian space programme was set up in an old Catholic church called St Mary Magdalene's Church. A cattle-shed was converted into a laboratory. The church has since been turned into a space museum.

To run the new space programme, Dr Vikram Sarabhai got together a small group of young men, all in their twenties. One of these youngsters was A.P.J. Abdul Kalam (on the right), who later became the President of India. Kalam and six others were sent to NASA to learn about sounding rockets in-depth.

The team returned to India in 1963 to launch *Nike-Apache*. They faced many challenges. When the whole rocket didn't fit in the transport truck, the young scientists even carried parts of the rocket on their bicycles!

In 1965, the second sounding rocket, called *Centaure,* was launched from Thumba. On 2 February 1968, the then prime minister, Indira Gandhi, formally dedicated the Thumba launching site to the UN, as the Thumba Equatorial Rocket Launching Station (TERLS). TERLS was India's first step in acquiring rocket technology.

Finally, the first India-made rocket was launched on 20 November 1967. Weighing 10 kg, the *Rohini-75* reached an altitude of only 4.2 km, but it set the stage for India's entry into the space club.

At first, rockets were built in the workshops of the Bhabha Atomic Research Centre (BARC) at Trombay, near Mumbai. But in 1971, a rocket-fabrication facility was built at Thumba.

ISRO

ISRO (Indian Space Research Organisation) was set up in 1969 to organise and execute India's space activities, including the development, launch and operation of rockets and satellites, and their applications. The organisation aims to use space technology and apply it to various tasks of national importance. In 1972, the Government of India set up the Space Commission and the Department of Space and brought ISRO under it.

123
Spacecraft Missions
Including 3 Nano Satellites and 1 Micro Satellite

95
Launch Missions
Including Scramjet-TD RLV-TD and Crew Escape System

15
Student Satellites

3
Re-entry Missions

432
Foreign Satellites
of 34 Countries

3
Satellites by Indian Private Players

* As of January 2024

VIKRAM SARABHAI SPACE CENTRE (VSSC)

Location:
Thiruvananthapuram

Operational Since:
21 November 1963

USP:
It is the lead centre for all rocket and launch vehicle programmes of ISRO.

Facilities:
All research and development activities related to satellite launch vehicle design and fabrication are carried out in Valiamala and Thumba.

Solid propellants for rockets are manufactured at the Propellant Fuel Complex at Thumba and the ammonium perchlorate plant at Aluva, north of Thiruvananthapuram.

ISRO also has a Liquid Propulsion Systems Centre, where liquid propulsion stages for the launch vehicles are developed. The test facilities are located at Mahendragiri, on the southern tip of Tamil Nadu.

U.R. RAO SATELLITE CENTRE (URSC)

Formerly Known As:
ISRO Satellite Centre (ISAC)

Location:
Bengaluru

Operational Since:
11 May 1972

USP:
It is the leading centre for building satellites and developing associated satellite technologies.

Facilities:
URSC has built more than 100 satellites for providing applications to users in the areas of communication, navigation, meteorology, remote sensing, space science and interplanetary explorations.

SPACE APPLICATIONS CENTRE (SAC)

Location:
Ahmedabad

Operational Since:
1972

USP:
It is the leading centre responsible for research and development on applications of space technology that are useful for people.

Facilities:
Its main areas of activity are satellite communication and remote sensing for Earth-resource applications such as communication, broadcasting, navigation, disaster-monitoring, meteorology and oceanography.

It also has facilities for spacecraft payload fabrication and testing.

SAC provides the communication transponders used to relay signals for telecommunication and television broadcasting. Each transponder is like a small relay station in space. It receives signals sent up from the large dish antennas on the ground at one frequency, amplifies them several hundred thousand times, and then beams them back at another frequency to the ground. They can later be received using a simple dish antenna, like the ones cable operators use, or a direct-to-home (DTH) antenna. Each *Indian National SATellite* (*INSAT*) and *Geostationary SATellite* (*GSAT*) carries several transponders, which are instrumental in reaching remote parts of the country.

SATISH DHAWAN SPACE CENTRE (SDSC)

Formerly Known As:

Sriharikota High Altitude Range (SHAR) In 2002 its name of was changed to commemorate Satish Dhawan, the former Chairman of ISRO.

Location:

Sriharikota

Operational Since:

1 October 1971

USP:

It is ISRO's main satellite-launching centre.

Facilities:

It has one launchpad for sounding rockets and two from where the rocket-launching operations of *Polar Satellite Launch Vehicle* (*PSLV*) and *Geostationary Satellite Launch Vehicle* (*GSLV*) are carried out.

Sriharikota Island (in Andhra Pradesh on the east coast) was chosen in 1969 to establish a satellite launching station. Satellites launched eastward from here get an additional boost of about 1,660 km/hour. Moreover, in case of any mishap, the debris of an east-bound large rocket can only fall into the sea. This minimises the risk of damage on land.

The new launch centre became operational in 1971, with the launch of an *RH-125* sounding rocket.

SATELLITES OF INDIA

Back in the 1970s, ISRO decided to master the technology of building satellites before designing and building rockets to launch them, primarily to gain time. The strategy has paid rich dividends, going by the experience of the past decades. Today, India is not only capable of designing and building the most sophisticated satellites but is a world leader in using satellites for economic and social development.

ARYABHATA

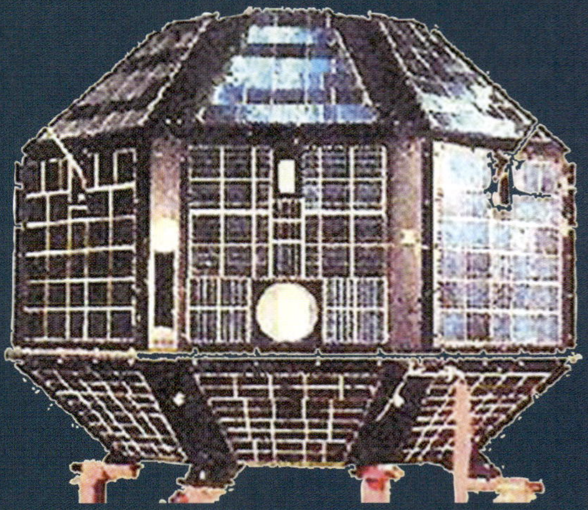

Type of Satellite: Experimental
Weight: 358 kg
Launched: 19 April 1975
Launch Site: Volgograd Launch Station (presently in Russia)
Launched By: Soviet Union
Mission Life: 6 years
Orbital Life: 17 years
Objective: To test technology
Achievements: India's first satellite

BHASKARA

Type of Satellite: Experimental Remote Sensing

Series: *Bhaskara-I* and *Bhaskara-II*

Weight: 444 kg (both)

Launched: 7 June 1979 and 20 November 1981

Launch Site: Volgograd Launch Station (presently in Russia)

Launched By: Soviet Union

Mission Life: 1 year (both)

Orbital Life: About 10 years (both)

Objective: For Earth observation and research in the areas of meteorology, hydrology, forestry and ocean surface studies

APPLE

(ARIANE PASSENGER PAYLOAD EXPERIMENT)

Type of Satellite: Experimental communication satellite

Weight: 670 kg

Launched: 19 June 1981

Launch Site: Kourou (CSG), French Guiana

Launched By: European Space Agency

Mission Life: 2 years

Orbital Life: 2 years

Objective: Used in several communications experiments, including the nationwide relay of TV programmes and radio networking

Achievements:

- The first indigenously built communication satellite
- Provided valuable experience in designing, building and operating geostationary communication satellites like the *INSAT-2* series

COMMUNICATION SATELLITES

These satellites are designed to transmit signals to the Earth. They are primarily used for broadcasting and distributing television signals to terrestrial broadcasting stations and to help with telecommunication.

INSAT

No. of Satellites Launched: 24

Type of Satellites: Geostationary multipurpose satellites

No. of Satellites Launched: 24

First Satellite Launch: April 1982 at Cape Canaveral Air Force Station (CCAFS) by NASA

Still in Service: 11

Objective: Telecommunication, broadcasting, meteorology and satellite-based search and rescue

Achievements:

- India's first multipurpose domestic satellite system, built to save costs
- Largest domestic communication satellite systems in the world (including *GSAT*), with 11 operational satellites in orbit
- Conceived as a three-in-one package, they provided reliable long-distance telecom services, round-the-clock weather observation and data-relay facility, and countrywide networking of All India Radio (AIR) and Doordarshan centres—all at the same time

GSAT

Type of Satellites: Communication satellites

First Satellite Launch: 18 April 2001 at Sriharikota by ISRO

No. of Satellites Launched: 20

Still in Service: 16

Objective: Used for digital audio, data and video broadcasting for both military and civilian use

Achievements:

- Largest domestic communication satellite systems in the world (including *INSAT*), with 16 operational satellites in orbit
- Made India self-reliant in broadcasting service

NOTABLE *GSAT* SATELLITES

GSAT-7

GSAT-7 or *INSAT-4F* is a multi-band military communications satellite developed by SRO. It has been operational since September 2013, and the Indian Navy is its prime user. *GSAT-7* communication payload is designed to provide communication capabilities to users over a vast oceanic region, including the Indian landmass.

GSAT-7A

GSAT-7A is an advanced military-communications satellite meant primarily for the Indian Air Force (IAF). It aims to enable the IAF to interlink different ground radar stations, the airbase, aircraft-to-aircraft real-time control systems, the Airborne Early Warning and Control System (AWACS) and the Defence Research and Development Organisation Airborne Early Warning and Control System (DRDO AEW&CS).

WEATHER WATCH

Apart from making countrywide communication and networking possible, the *INSAT*s have also revolutionised the way weathermen work. They enable round-the-clock monitoring of the weather. This allows better forecasts and the timely issuance of disaster warning for impending cyclones. The *INSATs* relay data received from 1,800 unmanned meteorological data-collection platforms. Meteorologists then use this data to make weather forecasts.

As part of an *INSAT*-based Cyclone Warning Dissemination System, about 250 special receivers have been installed in the cyclone-prone areas of Andhra Pradesh, north Tamil Nadu, Odisha, West Bengal and Gujarat. When a cyclone is likely to strike the coast, these receivers automatically send out alarms, alerting the residents and saving thousands of lives.

INDIA'S REMOTE-SENSING SATELLITES

India built its first operational remote-sensing satellite, the *IRS* series, in 1988. Since then, it has launched 24 remote-sensing satellites, out of which 13 are still functional. Currently, India has the largest constellation of operational remote-sensing satellites in the world. ISRO, through the National Remote-Sensing Centre (NRSC), Hyderabad, has been utilising the imagery from remote-sensing satellites and providing essential data for the planning and utilisation of natural resources over the past three decades.

IRS SERIES

Type of Satellite: Remote Sensing

Series: *IRS-1A* and *IRS-1B*

Weight: 975 kg (both)

Launched: 17 March 1988 and 19 August 1991

Launch Site: Baikanur Cosmodrome, Kazakhstan

Launched by: Former Soviet Union

Mission Life: 3 years (both)

Orbital Life: 8 years and 4 months; 12 years and 4 months

Objective: Recording, processing, data generation and analysis in a variety of application areas, such as agriculture, water resources, forestry, geology and hydrology etc.

Achievements:

- First of the series of indigenous state-of-the-art remote-sensing satellites.
- Marked the coming of age of India's satellites and their capability to address the various requirements for managing natural resources of the nation.

OTHER NOTABLE SATELLITES IN THE *IRS* SERIES

IRS-1C and *IRS-1D*: The second generation remote-sensing satellites, they are based on *IRS-1A* and *IRS-1B* satellites. Improvements and modifications were made to facilitate their launch using the Indian launch vehicle *PSLV*. Besides other features, they were equipped with the PAN camera that provides a better spatial resolution.

IRS-P6: The latest in the *IRS* series, this satellite has further enhanced capabilities, as compared to *IRS-1C* and *IRS-1D*. It carried out studies in areas of crop discrimination, crop yield, crop stress, pest/disease surveillance, disaster management etc.

OCEANSAT (*IRS-P4*): This satellite launched in May 1999 was meant for exclusive observation of the oceans and to help Indian fishermen identify rich fishing areas in India's coastal waters.

RESOURCESAT-2: The satellite contributes significantly to provide remote-sensing data services related to land and water resource management, and crop management and disaster management to global users.

CARTOSATs: This includes nine remote-sensing satellites carrying special cameras, the images from which are used for better mapmaking. Remote-sensing images received from the *IRS* satellites are of such high quality that they are in demand globally.

RISAT

Type of Satellite: Earth-observation satellites

Series: *RISAT-2; RISAT-1; Risat-2A*

Weight: 300 kg; 1,858 kg; 615 kg

Launched: 20 April 2009; 26 April 2012; 22 May 2019

Launch Site: SHAR Centre (later SDSC), Sriharikota

Launched By: ISRO, India

Launch Vehicle: *PSLV-C19; PSLV-XL* and *PSLV-C46*

Mission Life: 5 years

Orbital Life: Active

Objective: To sense or 'observe' the Earth using radar beams from space, day and night, and under cloudy conditions. The all-weather seeing feature makes the *RISAT*s special for security forces and disaster-relief agencies.

Achievements:

- It is the first all-weather Earth observation satellite from ISRO.
- The high-resolution pictures and microwave imaging from the *RISAT*s can also be used for defence surveillance. It can pick up structures and new bunkers so clearly that at times, it is even possible to count them.
- These satellites are being used for border surveillance, to deter insurgent infiltration and anti-terrorist operations as they can capture ground images when it is cloudy, raining or in the dark.
- They enable monitoring of crop health, particularly paddy monitoring in the Kharif season throughout the monsoon months when large parts of India remain under cloud cover.

EMISAT

(ELECTRO MAGNETIC INTELLIGENCE-GATHERING SATELLITE)

Type of Satellite: Surveillance satellite

Weight: 436 kg

Launched: 1 April 2019

Launch Site: SDSC, Sriharikota

Launched By: ISRO, India

Launch Vehicle: *PSLV*

Mission Life: 5 years

Objective: To detect, locate and characterise electromagnetic signals, such as those transmitted by military radars.

Achievements:

- India's first electronic surveillance satellite.
- Can provide location and information about hostile radars placed at the borders and adds strength to the armed forces.

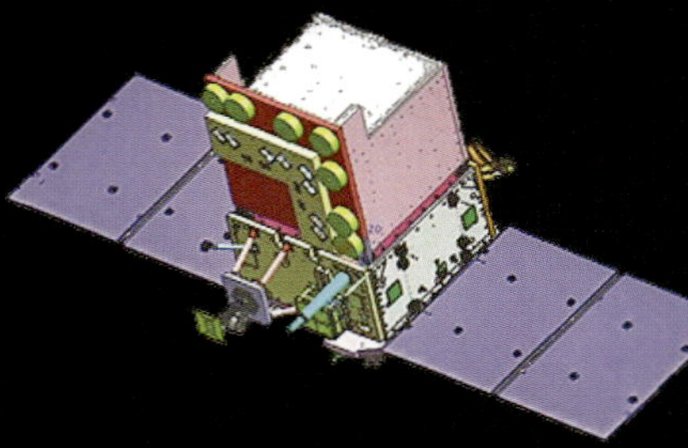

THE SOUTH ASIA SATELLITE

Type of Satellite: Geostationary communications and meteorology satellite

Also known as: *GSAT-9*

Weight: 436 kg

Launched: 7 May 2017

Launch Site: SDSC, Sriharikota

Launched By: ISRO, India

Launch Vehicle: *PSLV*

Mission Life: 5 years

Objective: To provide various communication applications to serve the needs of SAARC member nations.

Achievements:

The multidimensional facilities provided by the satellite are being used by six nations: Afghanistan, Bangladesh, Bhutan, the Maldives, Nepal and Sri Lanka. Pakistan chose not to join the project, citing that it was developing its own satellite.

KALPANA-1

Type of Satellite: Meteorological satellite

Originally known as: *METeorological SATellite (METSAT)*

Weight: 498 kg

Launched: 12 September 2002

Launch Site: SHAR Centre, Sriharikota

Launched By: ISRO, India

Launch Vehicle: *PSLV-C4*

Mission Life: 7 years

Orbital Life: 10+ years

Objective: The meteorological geostationary satellite was designed to study atmospheric cloud cover, water vapour and temperature data

Achievements:

- It was the first exclusively built meteorological satellite by ISRO.
- *METSAT* was a precursor to the later *INSAT* system, which had separate satellites for meteorology and telecommunication and broadcasting services.
- On 5 February 2003, *METSAT-1* was renamed *Kalpana-1* to honour the late Indian-born astronaut Kalpana Chawla, who died on 1 February 2003, when her space shuttle *Columbia* shattered in the skies over the US.

INDIAN SATELLITE LAUNCH VEHICLES

Large rockets that are used for launching satellites are known as satellite launch vehicles.

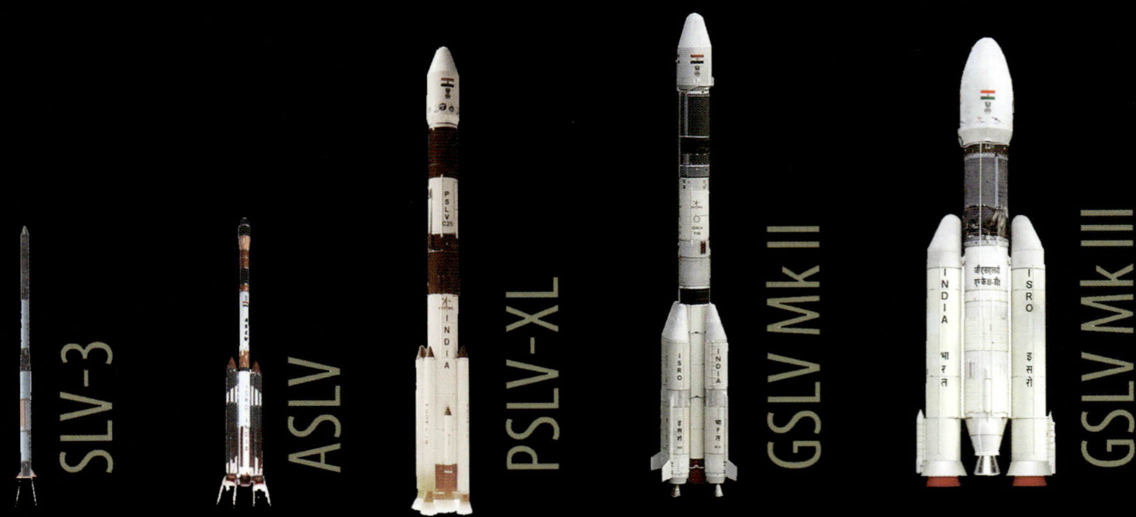

SLV-3
Height: 22.7m
Lift-off weight: 17t
Propulsion: All Solid
Payload mass: 40 kg
Orbit: Low-Earth Orbit

ASLV
Height: 23.Sm
Lift-off weight: 39t
Propulsion: All Solid
Payload mass: 150 kg
Orbit: Low-Earth Orbit

PSLV-XL
Height: 44m
Lift-off weight: 320t
Propulsion: Solid & Liquid
Payload mass: 1,860 kg
Orbit: 475 km Sun Synchronous Polar Orbit (1300 kg in Geosynchronous Transfer Orbit)

GSLV Mk II
Height: 49m
Lift-off weight: 414 t
Propulsion: Solid, Liquid & Cryogenic
Payload mass: 2,200 kg
Orbit: Geosynchronous Transfer Orbit

GSLV Mk III
Height: 43.43 m
Lift-off weight: 640 t
Propulsion: Solid, Liquid & Cryogenic
Payload mass: 4,000 kg
Orbit: Geosynchronous Transfer Orbit

A satellite launch vehicle is built in parts. Each part, referred to as a 'stage', is a rocket in itself. The use of stages in a satellite launch vehicle reduces fuel consumption, cuts down the satellite's weight, and helps propel it to higher altitudes. Traditionally, a one-piece rocket would be forced to carry the empty rocket case for a large part of the flight, causing unnecessary fuel wastage. It would also prevent the rocket from reaching the high speeds required to place a satellite in orbit.

In a launch vehicle, the stages are joined together one above the other. The lowermost rocket burns first, followed by the next on top and then the topmost, till all the stages burn out and fall away, leaving only the satellite in orbit. It is similar to a relay race, where the first runner passes on the baton to the next, and so on.

SLV-3

SLV-3 was India's first satellite launch vehicle. It was a four-stage rocket—22.7m tall, weighing 17 tonnes and entirely powered by solid propellants. Dr A.P.J. Abdul Kalam spearheaded the project.

*SLV-3*s first experimental flight was conducted in August 1979. But it was only partially successful. Then, on 18 July 1980, the first successful launch of *SLV-3* took place from the SHAR range. It carried the Indian-built satellite *Rohini-1* and placed it in a low-Earth orbit. Two more successful flights of the *SLV-3* took place on 31 May 1981 and 17 April 1983, carrying two more *Rohini* satellites to low-Earth orbits.

ASLV

The *Augmented Satellite Launch Vehicle* (*ASLV*) was a five-stage solid-fuel rocket developed by ISRO, built to place 150 kg satellites into low-Earth orbit. The *ASLV* was an augmented version of the *SLV-3*. The greater power of the *ASLV* came from two additional solid propellant boosters, which were strapped on to the main rocket body.

The first two flights of the *ASLV* on 24 March 1987 and 13 July 1988 did not succeed. The third developmental flight, *ASLV-D3*, on 20 May 1992, successfully placed a 106 kg satellite—*Stretched Rohini Series Satellite-C* (*SROSS-C*)—in a low-altitude (400 km) orbit. The fourth and last flight of the *ASLV* took place on 4 May 1994, which successfully placed the SROSS-C2 in a low-Earth orbit.

THE *PSLV*: ISRO'S WORKHORSE

The *Polar Satellite Launch Vehicle* (*PSLV*) is the next stage in the development of India's launch vehicles. It was the first Indian launch vehicle to be equipped with liquid stages. It is much bigger than the *ASLV* and was designed to carry heavier *IRS*-type satellites. The *PSLV* allowed India to launch its *IRS* satellites into polar orbits, a service that was commercially available only from Russia, earlier.

The *PSLV* undertook its first successful flight on 15 October 1994 from SHAR. It placed the 807 kg remote-sensing satellite, *IRS-P2*, in the polar orbit. With this success, India became the sixth nation in the world to attain the capability of launching satellites weighing up to 1,000 kg. It marked a significant milestone in India's march towards achieving self-reliance in satellite-launch capability.

Compared to the *SLV-3* and *ASLV*, the *PSLV* is a giant rocket—44 m tall, weighing 280 tonnes. It has four main stages and six solid-propellant strap-on boosters for additional power at launch.
The second and fourth stages use a liquid propellant-fuelled engine called 'Vikas', designed by ISRO.

The *PSLV* took two more successful flights on 21 March 1996 and 29 September 1997. This cleared the way for the first commercial flight of the rocket, on 26 May 1999, from SHAR. It carried three satellites—an *IRS* satellite *OCEANSAT*, a Korean satellite and a German satellite. It was the first time that an Indian launch vehicle was used to launch satellites of other countries.

The *PSLV* was also used to launch the 1,060 kg meteorological satellite *Kalpana-1* (*METSAT-1*) into geostationary transfer orbit in 2002.

104 SATELLITES IN A SINGLE FLIGHT

The *PSLV* holds the record for putting the largest number of satellites in orbit, in a single flight. In its 39th flight on 15 February 2017, *PSLV C-37* placed the remote-sensing satellite *CARTOSAT-2* and 103 smaller satellites, including 96 from the US, in orbit. In the 25 years since its first successful flight, the *PSLV* has turned out to be ISRO's most reliable workhorse, with 46 successful flights, out of 49. The *PSLV* has also been used to launch *Chandrayaan-1*, India's first mission to the Moon in 2008, its maiden mission to Mars *Mangalyaan* in 2013, and *CARTOSAT-3* in 2019.

THE *GSLV* TO THE GEOSTATIONARY ORBIT

The success of the *PSLV* was crucial for the next generation of larger Indian launch vehicle—the *Geosynchronous Satellite Launch Vehicle* (*GSLV*). The *GSLV* was developed primarily to launch satellites of the *INSAT* class, weighing up to 2,500 kg, into the geostationary transfer orbit.

The *GSLV* is a three-stage launch vehicle, with four liquid strap-on boosters. The first stage uses solid propellant and the second uses a Vikas engine. The third stage uses India's first cryogenic engine, developed under the Cryogenic Upper Stage Project.

The first demonstration flight of the *GSLV* took off from SHAR, Sriharikota on 18 April 2001, but the 1,540 kg satellite *GSAT-1* could not be placed in the geosynchronous orbit. The second flight took place on 8 May 2003 and successfully placed the *GSAT-2* in orbit.

GSLV

Height:
43.43 metres

Vehicle Diameter:
4 metres

Heat Shield (Payload Fairing) Diameter: 5 metres

Number of Stages: 3

CRYOGENIC ENGINES

Cryogenic engines, used for the first time in the *GSLV*, are a special kind of rocket engines. They can generate much more power for every kilogram of propellant used, than conventional solid or liquid propellant rocket engines. For the first five flights of the *GSLV*, cryogenic engines were obtained from Russia. Then, the supply and transfer of technology had to be stopped due to the Missile Technology Control Regime, which prohibits the proliferation of missiles and missile technology. So, ISRO had to develop its own cryogenic engine for use in *GSLV*s.

The first operational flight of *GSLV* was the launch of the *EDUSAT* communications satellite on 20 September 2004. On 19 December 2018, the *GSLV* was used to launch *GSAT-7A* into the geosynchronous transfer orbit.

The main objective of India's five-and-a-half-decade-old space programme has been to bring the benefits of space technology to the common man. ISRO tasted the fruits of space technology even before it could build its own communication satellites. The first India-wide television broadcast using a satellite happened in 1975, long before the launch of its first communication satellite.

SATELLITE INSTRUCTIONAL TELEVISION EXPERIMENT (SITE)

The tremendous power of space technology was amply demonstrated by a year-long experimental project called SITE, which made use of NASA's first direct broadcasting satellite, *ATS-6.* The satellite could broadcast television programmes directly to special receiving sets equipped with small dish antennas. It was borrowed from NASA starting 1 August 1975 to 31 July 1976.

SITE's main objective was to understand how satellite television could be used as a medium of mass education in a vast country like India. Under the project, a total of 2,400 villages—400 each in Andhra Pradesh, Bihar, Karnataka, Madhya Pradesh, Odisha and Rajasthan—were each given a direct broadcast receiving set, developed at SAC in Ahmedabad.

Despite its limited duration, SITE was hailed as a success. It demonstrated the benefits of using space technology for human resource development. Today, DTH services are available everywhere. People living in the remotest corner of the country can watch any TV channel sitting at home, thanks to the power of space technology.

In 1975, only five cities in the country had television stations. Yet, because of SITE, people in 2,400 villages could watch TV in their villages. The programmes telecast during SITE mainly covered topics—such as farming, health, family welfare and education—that interested the local people. So people in the villages not only enjoyed the thrill of being able to watch TV but also loved the programmes aired!

SATELLITE TELECOMMUNICATION EXPERIMENTAL PROJECT (STEP)

Soon after SITE ended, ISRO undertook another experimental project involving satellite communication, in collaboration with the Post and Telegraphs Department. The Satellite Telecommunication Experimental Project (STEP), which was conducted for two years from 1 January 1977 to 1 January 1979, using a Franco-German satellite called *Symphonie*.

STEP provided Indian scientists valuable experience in making use of satellite channels for ground-based telecom networks. Two terminals were built during the project—a road transportable terminal and a small terminal that could be airlifted. These were used to demonstrate the use of satellite communication in remote areas and emergencies. We can see such transportable terminals atop media vans (OB vans).

Together, SITE and STEP provided valuable experience to Indian space scientists in satellite applications. This further helped them make the most of the *INSAT*s when they were commissioned in the 1980s. Today, the *INSAT*s and *GSAT*s form the backbone of India's vast telecommunication network and are an important part of its meteorological network. It is because of satellite-based networks that we can withdraw money from our bank account at any ATM across the country and carry out online transactions from anywhere.

HOME ENTERTAINMENT

The *INSATs* have been a catalyst in the rapid expansion of television coverage in India. More than 900 million people in India now have access to TV, through approximately 1,400 terrestrial rebroadcast transmitters. Television has reached even the remotest parts of the country, like the Andaman and Nicobar Islands. People can watch programmes in their own languages from anywhere, thanks to Doordarshan's regional satellite channels.

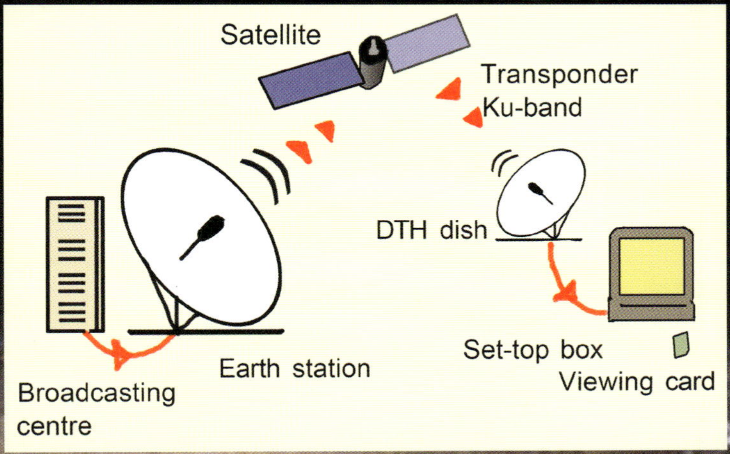

The *INSATs* also provide radio networking facility for almost 440 stations of AIR, providing high-quality broadcasts to millions of listeners.

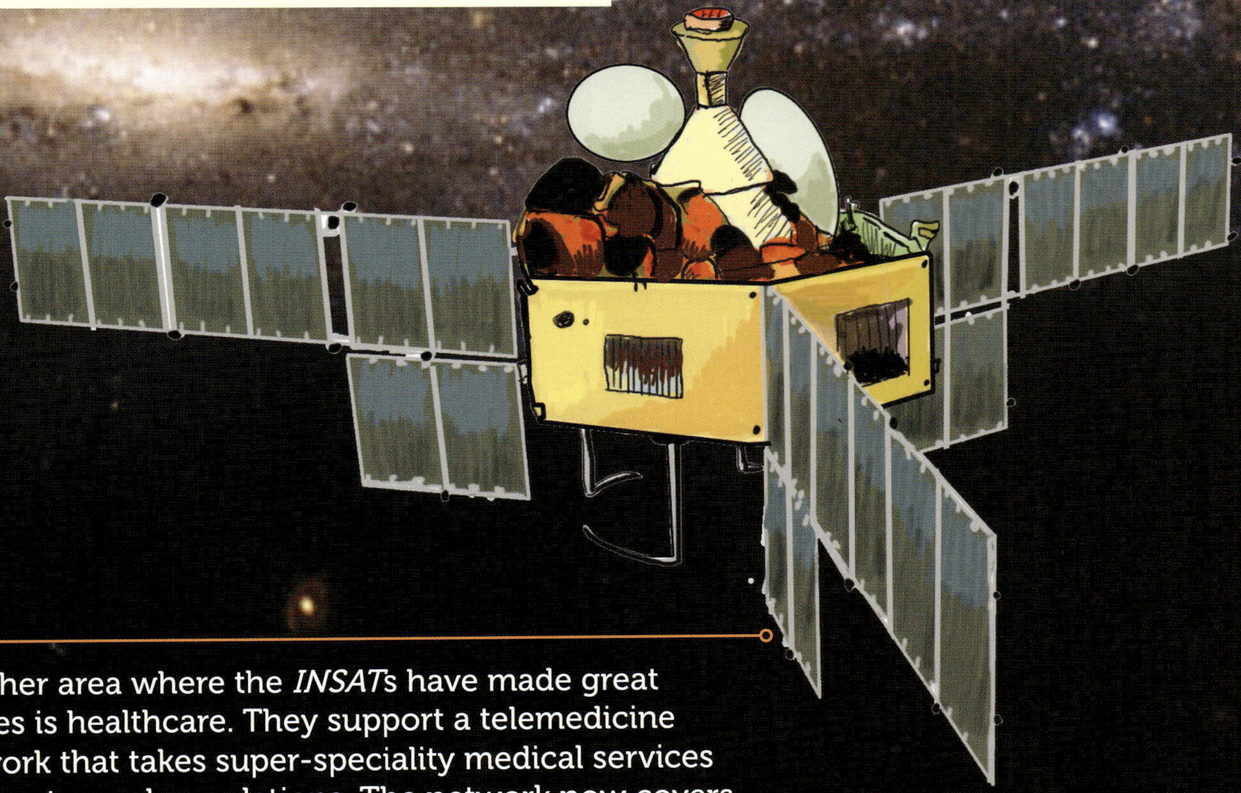

Another area where the *INSATs* have made great strides is healthcare. They support a telemedicine network that takes super-speciality medical services to remote rural populations. The network now covers 152 hospitals—120 remote rural hospitals and 32 super-speciality hospitals in major cities.

INDIA'S OWN GPS

Many of us use the Global Positioning System, or GPS, on our mobile phones to identify our position or find our way to a new location. Until recently, the US-based GPS and Russia's GLONASS were the only satellite-based navigation systems. But now, India has set up its own satellite-based navigation system.

The Indian system uses seven satellites in geosynchronous orbit, known as the Indian Regional Navigational Satellite System (IRNSS). They provide accurate positioning services across India and up to 1,500 km beyond its borders, with an accuracy of better than 5 metres. IRNSS has been renamed NAVIC (NAVigation using Indian Constellation). The name is apt, because NAVIC means 'sailor' or 'navigator' in Sanskrit, Hindi and many other Indian languages.

Three of the satellites in the NAVIC system are placed directly over the equator. They are placed in the geostationary orbit, so they appear static from the ground. The remaining four satellites are in pairs, placed in two inclined geosynchronous orbits. From the Earth, these satellites appear to follow a 'figure of eight' path in the sky.

Unlike the GPS and GLONASS, which use 24 satellites each, the Indian system is based on a constellation of only seven satellites. All seven are placed at a height of approximately 35,800 km, which makes them circle the Earth once every 24 hours, making them always accessible.

The NAVIC system provides navigation services on land, sea and air and helps in disaster and fleet management. Like GPS, the services of NAVIC are accessible using mobile phones. An advantage of the Indian system is that the design of the payload makes the NAVIC system compatible with the existing GPS.

MOON MISSIONS

The Moon is 3,84,400 km away from the Earth—more than ten times farther away than the geostationary orbit. When Vikram Sarabhai visualised India's space programme, he probably never thought of any mission beyond putting satellites in the Earth's orbit.

MISSION AIMS

1 To carry out a detailed 3D mapping of the Moon to understand the physical features and the chemical, radioactive and mineral makeup of the lunar rocks and soil.

2 To search for Helium-3, an isotope of helium, that could be a potential source of clean nuclear energy.

3 To look for water on the Moon.

CHANDRAYAAN-1

It was the first Indian mission to send back data and images of the entire lunar surface. The mission was named 'Chandrayaan' by the former Prime Minister Atal Bihari Vajpayee; the Sanskrit word means 'moon vehicle'.

FINDINGS

- Presence of water (H_2O) and hydroxyl (OH–), with water more abundant near the polar region.
- Presence of magnesium, iron, aluminium, silicon and calcium.
- New types of rock, with an unusual combination of minerals on the far side of the Moon.

LAUNCHED

On 22 October 2008, from SDSC, by *PSLV-C11*.

WEIGHT

Approx. 1,400 kg at the time of launch

STATUS

ISRO scientists lost contact with *Chandrayaan-1* in August 2009. In March 2017, scientists at NASA's Jet Propulsion Laboratory (JPL) in California, USA, located the spacecraft still circling some 200 km above the lunar surface.

CONSTRUCTION

A small spacecraft shaped like a large cube, powered by a single solar panel and a lithium-ion battery in the absence of sunlight

SPECIAL FEATURE

A detachable unit called the *Moon Impact Probe* was released after the spacecraft went into its assigned orbit around the Moon. Even though the *Chandrayaan*'s probe crashed upon landing, the probe managed to send back valuable images and data.

PAYLOAD

11

HIGHLIGHTS

- *Chandrayaan-1* reached the moon on 8 November 2008 but released its Moon Impact Probe on November 14, which crashed into the Moon on the same day.
- It beamed its first images of the Earth, specially India, on 25 March 2009.
- Although *Chandrayaan-1* successfully operated for 312 days and achieved around 95 per cent of its objectives.

CHANDRAYAAN-2

ndia's second mission to the Moon, an advanced version of *Chandrayaan-1*, aims at studying the entire Moon—areas combining the exosphere, the surface and sub-surface of the Moon.

PAYLOAD

13, eight on the orbiter, three on the lander and two on the rover.

STATUS

On 7 September 2019, the landing sequence of *Vikram* lander carrying the *Pragyan* rover started perfectly and was going smooth till a few minutes before the touchdown when it lost contact, suddenly. ISRO later said Vikram probably made a 'hard' landing and may have been damaged. The debris of the *Vikram* lander was also spotted on the Moon surface. However, the *Chandrayaan-2* orbiter, is performing well and is expected to remain in orbit for more than seven years.

LAUNCHED

On 22 July 2019, from SDSC, by *GSLV Mk-III*.

WEIGHT

3,877 kg, the heaviest payload ever launched from Indian soil.

CONSTRUCTION

Consists of three components: an orbiter, a lander and a rover.

THE ORBITER

- It carries scientific payloads.
- It orbits around the Moon.
- And it also carries out mapping from an altitude of 100 km.

THE LANDER: *VIKRAM*

Named in honour of the Indian scientist Vikram Sarabhai

- It carries the rover to the Moon's surface
- It serves as a communication relay between the rover, orbiter and the Earth.
- It carries instruments to conduct three scientific experiments and take measurements after landing.

THE ROVER: *PRAGYAN*

- Is a six-wheeled robotic vehicle designed to move autonomously within a 500 m radius of the landing site.
- Is equipped with a 50 watt solar panel for powering its propulsion system, scientific instruments and communication equipment
- Its mission life is limited to one lunar day, or 14 Earth days

ISRO released the first set of data from the mission in December 2020, nearly a year after its launch.

DID YOU KNOW

A camera onboard Chandrayaan–2 captured the Sarabhai Crater on a lunar mare region, called Mare Serenitatis, which has vast lava plains. The crater, named after the famous astrophysicist Dr. Vikram Sarabhai, lies approximately 250-300 km west to the landing site of *Apollo 17* and *Luna 21* missions.

The primary objective of the mission was to demonstrate the ability to soft-land on the lunar surface and operate a robotic rover on the surface. The landing spot selected for *Chandrayaan-2*'s lander-rover was about 600 km from the lunar South Pole, which is the farthest from the equator that any lunar mission has attempted before. This is significant because the lunar surface area, which remains in shadow, is much larger here than that at the North Pole. This signals a possibility of the presence of water in permanently shadowed areas around it. In addition, the South Pole region has craters that are cold traps and contain a fossil record of the early solar system.

CHANDRAYAAN-3

Chandrayaan-3 is the third and latest mission in the series by ISRO, launched to explore the Moon and demonstrate its capability in safe landing and roving on the lunar surface.

WEIGHT

3,895 kilograms

LAUNCHED

On 14 July 2023, at 2:35 pm IST from the Satish Dhawan Space Centre in Sriharikota.

STATUS

The spacecraft successfully aced the fourth orbit-raising manoeuvres around the Earth. The lander and the rover landed on the Moon on 23 August 2023, near the lunar south pole region. With this, India joined an exclusive club of three nations—the United States, the erstwhile Soviet Union and China—that have accomplished a soft landing on the Moon. Japan is the latest entrant to an exclusive four-nation club, with a successful soft landing on the Moon, in January 2024.

LAUNCH VEHICLE

LVM3 is a heavy-lift launch vehicle that is 43.5 metres tall with a diameter of 4 meters and a lift-off mass of 640 tonnes. The LVM-3 utilises a cryogenic upper stage powered by CE-20, India's largest cryogenic engine, enabling it to carry heavier payloads. It also incorporates two S200 solid rocket boosters and two L110 liquid-stage Vikas rockets for additional thrust during takeoff.

COMPONENTS

Consists of three components: an indigenous Lander module (LM), Propulsion module (PM) and a Rover. The Lander Module will be responsible for the soft landing on the lunar surface. The Propulsion module will help provide propulsion and attitude control for the entire mission. And the rover will explore the lunar surface and collect scientific data.

THE GOAL

- To place a lander and rover on the lunar surface for one lunar day, which is 14 Earth days.

PAYLOAD

Chandrayaan-3 has six payloads—four on the lander and two on the rover.

TECHNOLOGY

- The technologies on the spacecraft include laser and RF-based altimeters, velocimeters, throttleable liquid engines, hazard detection and avoidance systems, and a landing leg mechanism.

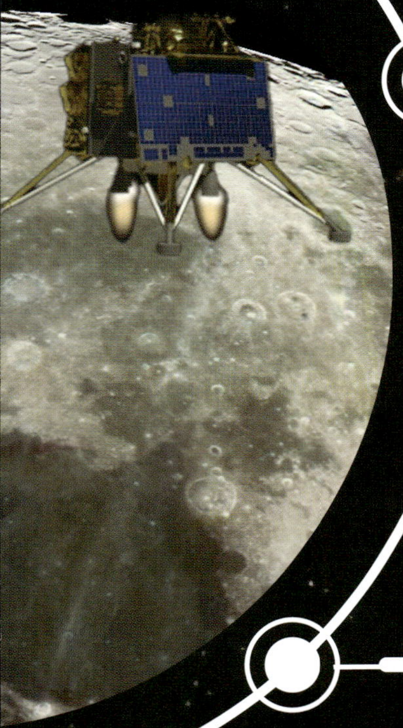

MISSION OBJECTIVES

- Soft-landing of the mission's rover on the lunar surface. With this, India also became the first country to land on the moon's south pole.
- Demonstrating the rover's capability of exploring the lunar surfaces.
- Conducting scientific experiments including studying lunar ice formations in craters. If successful, the mission could be the first to collect lunar ice samples.
- Gathering valuable scientific data to understand and contribute to the advancement of lunar research.

COST OF THE MISSION

₹ 615 crore

IMPROVEMENT

Unlike *Chandrayaan-2*, the *Chandrayaan-3* is an improved version for better performance. Some of these include:

- It has no orbiter or secondary payloads to focus on the lander and rover.
- The lander is now better equipped to handle higher velocities of landing.
- Adding a bi-propellant propulsion system with more propellant and solar power will help handle fluctuations in fuel levels and other uncertainties.
- It also contains improved software, control and guidance algorithms.

MANGALYAAN

The *Mars Orbiter Mission* (MOM) or the *Mangalyaan* is India's first interplanetary space probe. It entered the Mars orbit on 24 September 2014 and is the world's most economical mission to the Red Planet. It outlived its life-span of six months, living for about eight years in the Martian orbit. *Mangalyaan* provided several insights regarding the Martian surface's features, morphology, as well as the Martian atmosphere and exosphere.

MISSION ACCOMPLISHED

1. India's debut Mars mission threw light on the gases in the Martian atmosphere. It found the presence of suprathermal Argon-40 atoms in the Martian exosphere.
2. The probe discovered dust storms, the presence of clouds above the southern wall of Valles Marineris and studied the polar ice caps on the Red Planet.
3. The colour camera aboard the mission captured the complete disc image of Mars and helped generate its atlas.
4. The probe even photographed the far side of Deimos, one of the moons of Mars, for the first time.
5. Most interestingly, it looked beyond Mars and studied the Sun's Corona.

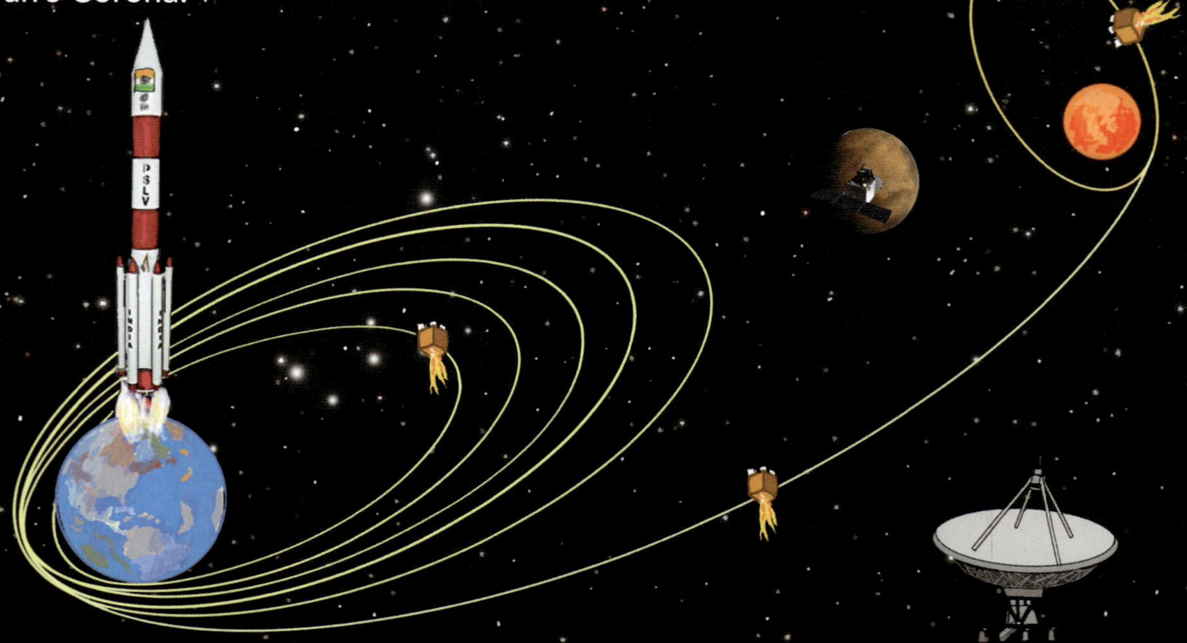

MARS ORBITER MISSION (MOM) OR MANGALYAAN

India's first interplanetary mission, *MOM* was meant to place a small probe in the Mars orbit.

CONSTRUCTION

This consists of an orbital craft equipped with five tools for the observation and study of Martian land and the atmosphere. These tools include Mars Colour Camera, Thermal Infrared Imaging Spectrometer, Methane Sensor for Mars, Mars Exospheric Neutral Composition Analyser and Lyman Alpha Photometer.

LAUNCHED

On 5 November 2013, from SDSC, by *PSLV*

ENTERED THE MARS ORBIT

On 24 September 2014

STATUS

Mangalyaan completed about eight years in Mars orbit in April 2022, well beyond its designed mission life of six months. The Mars Orbiter lost communication with the ground station and the mission 'attained end-of-life', as confirmed by ISRO, on 3 October 2022.

ACHIEVEMENTS

- *Mangalyaan* entered the Mars orbit in its maiden attempt! No other country has been able to succeed in their first attempt till now, and more than half of all Mars missions so far have failed.
- The spacecraft has been sending back stunning images and other scientific data. ISRO's Scientific Mars Atlas provides glimpses of the various features and atmospheric phenomenon occurring on Mars as captured by the Mars Colour Camera onboard *Mangalyaan*.
- The technological capability and the knowledge gained will be invaluable in future launches and operations and in the training of ISRO's flight operations and mission-control staff.

PAYLOAD

5

WEIGHT

1,337 kg

Mars is also called the red planet because it appears reddish due to the presence of iron oxide in the ground.

Minimum-Energy Launch Windows
For a mission to Mars, the timing of the launch is crucial because the red planet comes nearest to the Earth only once in 26 months. Fuel can be saved if launched at the right time. In recent years, there have been only three minimum-energy launch windows: November 2013 to January 2014; January 2016 to April 2016; and April 2018 to May 2018. ISRO availed the earliest one available in 2018!

Made in India
India's *MOM* was completely indigenous—built entirely by ISRO scientists—including the five scientific payloads onboard.

Special Launch Method
Initially, the *Mangalyaan* mission was to be launched by the *GSLV*. But the *GSLV* had failed twice in 2010, so the *PSLV* was used for the launch. Since the *PSLV* was not powerful enough to place *Mangalyaan* on a direct-to-Mars trajectory, the spacecraft was first launched into an Earth orbit. It then used its own thrusters and the Earth's gravity for orbit-raising to enter a trans-Mars trajectory.

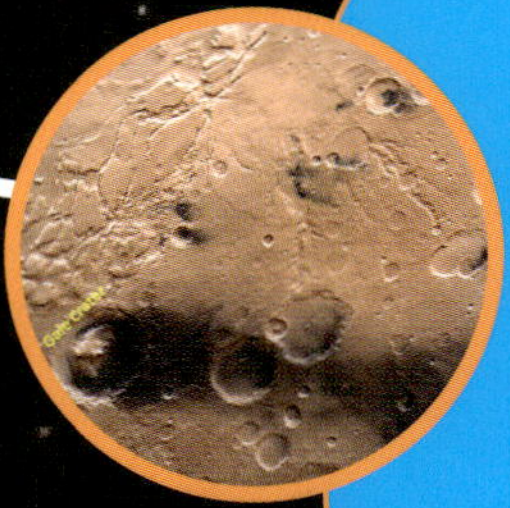

Manoeuvres in the Dark
After its launch, several in-orbit procedures were carried out for 300 days. *Mangalyaan* was then successfully inserted into a highly elliptical orbit around Mars, with farthest and nearest orbital points of approximately 80,000 km and 500 km, respectively. The probe manoeuvred into the orbit with precision, even when the spacecraft was on the other side of Mars, out of communication with the Earth. This was a remarkable achievement for ISRO scientists.

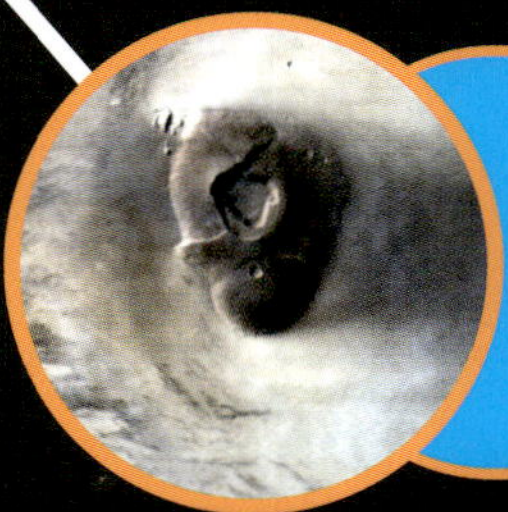

Looking for Methane
Mangalyaan carried the Methane Sensor for Mars to measure methane in the atmosphere, one of the hottest topics in Mars research. Unfortunately, it didn't work.

Economy Ticket to Mars
The Indian mission cost only one-ninth of the cost of the MAVEN mission of NASA, which had arrived at the red planet two days earlier before *Mangalyaan* touched down. It cost even less than the make-believe Hollywood movie *Gravity*!

ADITYA-L1

Aditya-L1 is ISRO's first space based observatory to study the Sun from a halo orbit around first Sun-Earth Lagrangian point (L1).

Mission Aims and Objectives:

- To study various Sun-activity-related phenomena, including solar photosphere, chromosphere and corona, in near-infrared, optical, X-ray and ultraviolet spectrum.
- To measure the magnitude and the nature of the interplanetary magnetic field.
- To achieve a fundamental understanding of the physical processes that heat the solar corona, accelerate solar wind and produce coronal mass ejections.

- To understand the dynamic processes of the Sun and address some outstanding problems in solar physics and heliophysics, i.e., the study of the effects of the Sun on the solar system.
- To help understand and predict climate change on the Earth.

CONSTRUCTION

Weighing 1,500 kg, satellite *Aditya-L1* carries seven science payloads, such as the Visible Emission Coronagraph, Solar Ultraviolet Imaging Telescope (SUIT) and magnetometer.

LAUNCH

On 2 September 2023, the Polar Satellite Launch Vehicle (PSLV-C57) successfully launched the *Aditya-L1* spacecraft, from Satish Dhawan Space Centre (SDSC), Sriharikota.

ORBIT

The Sun-Earth Lagrangian point L1, about 1.5 million km from the Earth. This allows the satellite to view the Sun, without any occultations or eclipses, continuously.

STATUS

The *Aditya-L1* spacecraft successfully completed four earth-bound orbital manoeuvres before entering the transfer orbit en route to the Lagrange point L1. After 128 days the solar observatory spacecraft reached its intended orbit at the L1 point on 6 January 2024 after Halo-Orbit Insertion (HOI).

ISRO'S COMMERCIAL SUCCESS

ISRO has been active in exploiting its launch capability to earn foreign exchange. Antrix Corporation Limited is a commercial arm of ISRO that is engaged in the promotion and commercial exploitation of space products, technical consultancy services and transfer of technologies developed by ISRO. Antrix markets *Indian Remote-Sensing* (*IRS*) Satellite data at very competitive costs globally. NewSpace India Limited (NSIL) is the other commercial arm of ISRO, entrusted with commercially exploiting the R&D work of the space agency and co-producing *PSLV* and launch satellites through small satellite launch vehicles (*SSLV*s). As of January 2023, ISRO had launched a total of 385 foreign satellites, most of them from the US, earning a total revenue of more than Rs 6,300 crore, which is expected to increase in the coming years.

GAGANYAAN

On 15 August 2018, Prime Minister Narendra Modi announced the launch of India's first human mission in 2022, the country's 75th year of Independence. However, after several delays due to Covid-19, India's first human mission, *Gaganyaan*, is expected to be launched by the end of 2024. The three-stage heavy-lift launch vehicle, *GSLV Mk-III*, has been selected to send three astronauts into a low-Earth orbit of 300–400 km for seven days. The mission, which literally means 'sky vehicle', will make India the fourth nation to launch a manned space flight after Russia, the US and China.

INDIGENOUS SPACESUIT

An indigenous spacesuit has been developed for Indian astronauts. The bright orange spacesuit is made of four layers and weighs less than 5 kg. It was developed at the VSSC in Thiruvananthapuram. Each spacesuit is equipped with an oxygen cylinder that can support an astronaut for up to 60 minutes. The Indian spacesuit is about 20 per cent lighter and 1/100 times cheaper than other spacesuits so far.

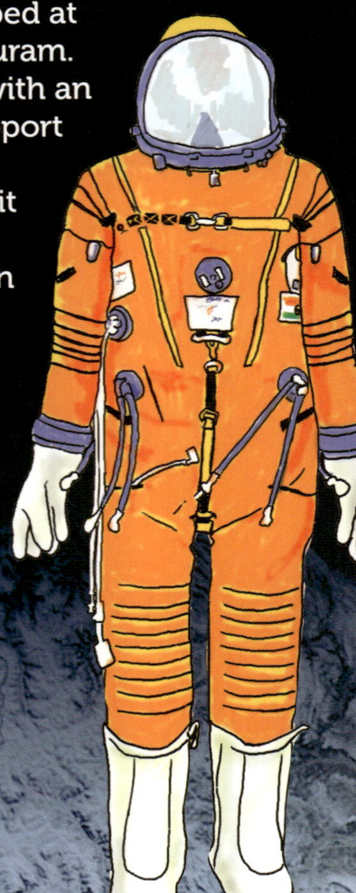

THE CREW MODULE

ISRO scientists have been working on designs and logistics of a space capsule, which will carry Indian astronauts to the Earth orbit and bring them back. The space capsule, jointly made by ISRO and Hindustan Aeronautics Limited (HAL), will carry three people and a planned upgraded version will be equipped with rendezvous and docking capability. The capsule will consist of two units—crew module and service module—and will have the capacity to carry two or three persons to a 400 km high orbit and return to a predetermined location in the sea.

MISSION PLAN

The mission duration will be up to seven days. The crew module will be equipped with a radiation-protection system, life-support system, waste-management system and thermal-protection system. Before re-entry into the atmosphere, the service module and solar panels will be discarded. The crew module will splashdown in the Bay of Bengal with the help of parachutes.

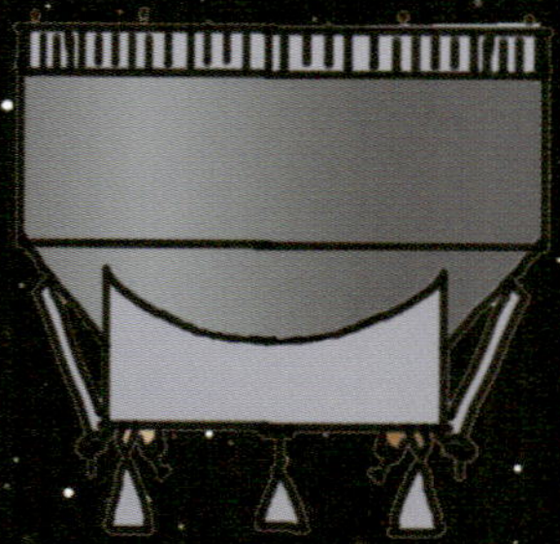

MISSION SCHEDULE

Two unmanned missions, which will carry the crew module with dummy passengers and scientific experiments are to be launched. The first unmanned launch was scheduled for December 2020, and the second six months after the first. However, due to the COVID-19 pandemic the first series of tests flights were launched on 21 October 2023. The first flight carrying Indian astronauts will now be launched with ISRO's *GSLV Mk-III* in 2025.

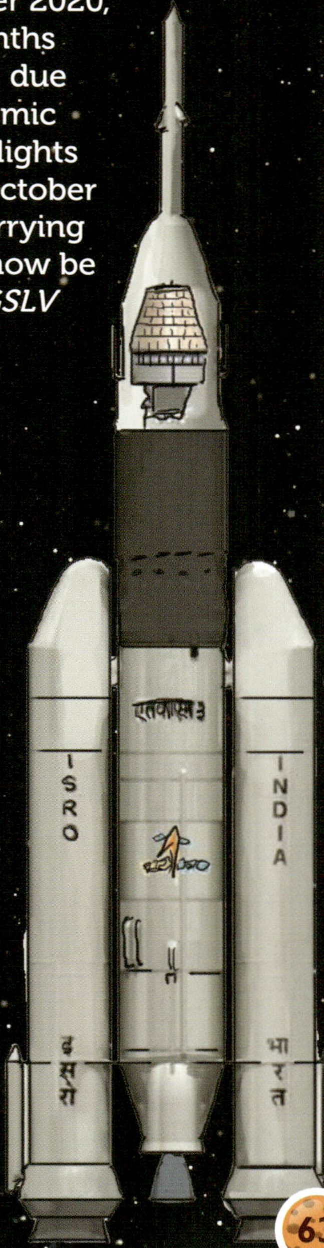

CREW SELECTION

The first level of selection for Indian astronauts for *Gaganyaan* was completed in September 2019 at the Institute of Aerospace Medicine, Bengaluru, with the selection of 12 Indian Air Force officers. Out of them, four officers were finally selected for training in Russia, which they completed in August 2020. As per a US-India agreement, signed in June 2023, Indian astronauts will now receive training in the US for a proposed flight to the International Space Station. This will help them with the preparations for *Gaganyaan*.

HUMAN SPACE FLIGHT CENTRE

ISRO has already set up a Human Space Flight Centre in the ISRO headquarters campus in Bengaluru and a management structure for the manned space programme. The *Gaganyaan* project, which has a budget of around Rs 10,000 crore, will function as a system under this new centre. The first meeting of the Gaganyaan National Advisory Council was held in June 2019. Many essential aspects were discussed, especially life-support systems, crew selection and training.

ATMOSPHERIC RE-ENTRY EXPERIMENTS

A crucial phase of any manned space flight is the re-entry of the crew module into the Earth's atmosphere from space, when it experiences extremely high temperatures. ISRO has conducted a couple of experiments to test its capability to protect the crew in this phase. A Space Capsule Recovery Experiment (SRE) was held in 2007 to test ISRO's re-entry technology. A 550 kg capsule was sent into orbit. The capsule was launched into a 635 km polar orbit on 10 January 2007 as a co-passenger with *CARTOSAT-2*. It stayed in orbit for 12 days, and its payloads performed all operations successfully. The SRE capsule returned to the Earth on 22 January 2007. A second experiment called Crew Module Atmospheric Re-entry Experiment (CARE) was conducted on 18 December 2014. A 3,745 kg space capsule—a prototype of what will be used by the Indian astronauts—was launched aboard *GSLV Mk-III* and separated from the launch vehicle at an altitude of 126 km. The crew module entered the atmosphere and parachuted down. It was safely recovered from the Bay of Bengal.

PAD ABORT TEST

During the launch, the crew module with astronauts inside will sit atop the launch vehicle. So, if there is any problem with the rocket after the first stage is ignited, the crew must be quickly moved to safety. This is done using a 'pad abort', where the crew module is separated and ejected to safety by small rockets. The crew module later parachutes down. ISRO successfully carried out the pad abort or crew escape test using a 12.5 tonne crew module at Sriharikota in July 2018.

THE HUMANOID ABOARD

A half-humanoid, Vyommitra, will ride *Gaganyaan's* first test flight. With just a torso and no legs Vyommitra can switch panel operations, manage the environment control and life support systems, speak with the astronauts and respond to their queries. The humanoid will simulate the human functions required for space before real astronauts take off.

BUDGET-FRIENDLY MISSION!

The Indian mission is expected to cost less than Rs 10,000 crore, which would be cheaper than similar projects undertaken by the US and China.

INDIAN DEEP SPACE NETWORK

The Indian Deep Space Network (IDSN), commissioned during 2008, forms the ground segment that provides deep space support for India's Space Science Missions, such as *Chandrayaan-1* and *MOM*. Indian Space Science Data Centre (ISSDC), located at the IDSN campus, is the primary data centre for data archives of Indian Space Science Missions. IDSN performed the important task of receiving the radio signals transmitted by *Chandrayaan-1* and sending commands to the spacecraft. The facility was also used for communication during India's maiden mission to Mars in 2013–14 and the *Chandrayaan-2* mission in 2019.

Looking forward, ISRO has several missions lined up in the near future. These include interplanetary missions to Venus and Mars, a probe to the Sun and *Chandrayaan-3*, the third mission to the Moon.

MANGALYAAN-2

This will be ISRO's second mission to Mars.

Mission Aim and Objectives:

- To conduct a study of methane emission
- To study Martian dust and its ionosphere

Scheduled for Launch: Approximately 2024–25, using the *GSLV Mk-III* (still being developed)

Construction: *Mangalyaan-2* will carry a lander and a rover with scientific experiments as additional payloads.

SHUKRAYAAN

The *Shukrayaan* will be ISRO's mission to Venus, the Earth's 'twin sister'. Since Venus and the Earth have similarities in terms of sizes, densities, composition and gravity, some scientists theorise that both planets may share a common origin and may have been formed at the same time from the same condensing swirl of gas and dust 4.5 billion years ago. Being 30 per cent closer to the Sun than the Earth, Venus is exposed to much higher levels of solar radiation, effects of solar flares and other solar phenomena, which makes it an object of interest for ISRO to study.

Mission Aims and Objectives:

- To study the atmosphere of Venus, which is made up primarily of carbon dioxide
- To study the dense, hot atmosphere of Venus and the planet's surface using a probe

Scheduled for Launch: December 2024 or 2026

Construction: This orbiter mission is still in the initial stages of planning. The objectives will decide the design of the spacecraft, including the 'super-rotation' of Venus's atmosphere and how it interacts with solar radiation and solar wind.

XPOSAT

The *ASTROSAT* was India's first dedicated multi-wavelength space telescope. It was launched in 2015 and was a success. ISRO has now decided to launch another astronomical mission—the *X-Ray Polarimeter Satellite* (or *XPOSAT*).

Scheduled for Launch: Late 2023

Mission Aim and Objectives:

- To further explore X-rays in the universe
- To study the angle of polarisation of bright X-ray sources in our universe

X-rays are emitted by neutron stars, supernova remnants, pulsars and regions around black holes, and studying them could give scientists information about the electromagnetic nature of space radiation. Understanding space radiation better could be used to protect spacecraft and astronauts in the future and also pave the way to understand the happenings in the universe better.

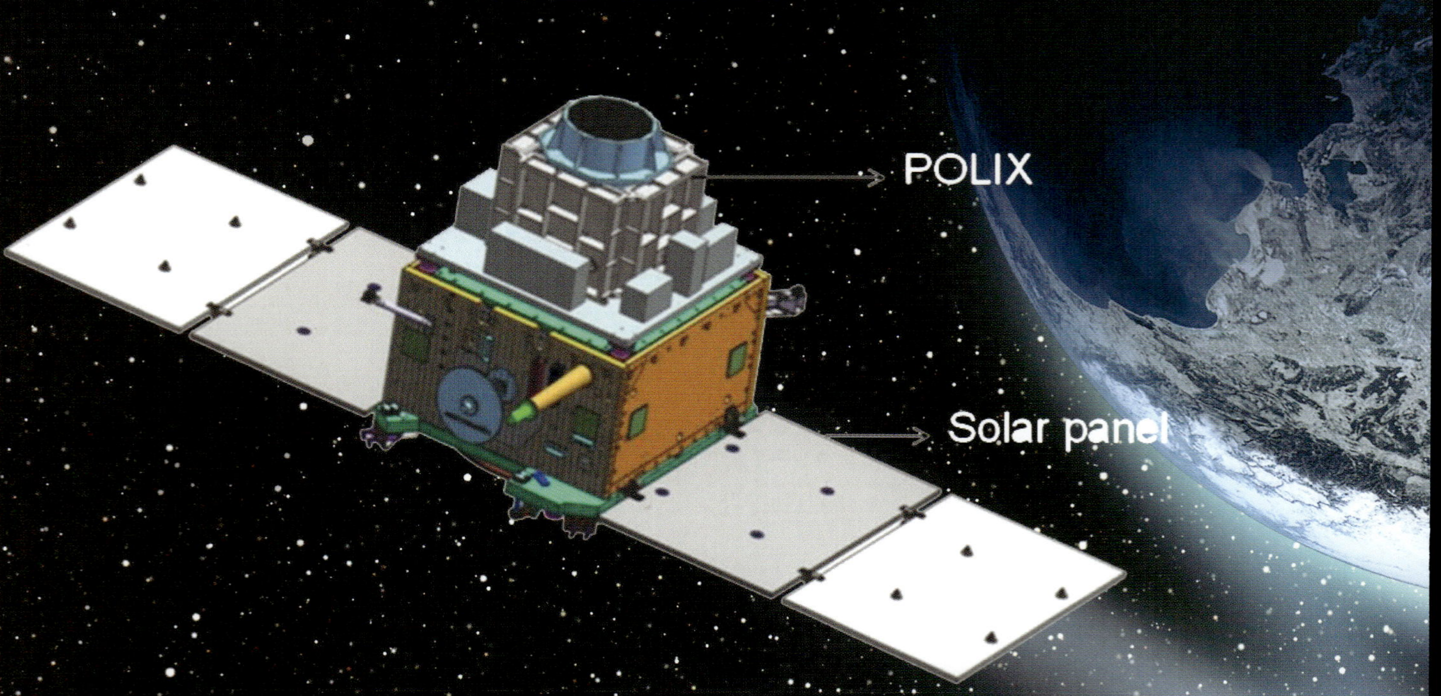

AN INDIAN SPACE STATION

The International Space Station, currently the only functioning one, is supposed to wind up by 2028. At a press conference in June 2019, ISRO chief, K. Sivan, announced the plan to create an Indian Space Station. The proposed Indian station will be a small module, weighing 15–20 tonnes. It will be able to host a small crew for 15–20 days.

The space station is being seen as a logical extension of the *Gaganyaan* mission that will send Indians to space in the end of 2024 or early 2025. The *Gaganyaan* will consist of a crew module and service module that will together constitute the orbital module weighing about 7 tonnes. Two liquid-propellant engines will power the service module. During the mission, the crew will do microgravity experiments. The modalities for it will be worked out after the first manned mission.

The timeline for the mission is five to seven years, which may be a tough challenge, but ISRO has been developing the necessary technologies, like the space-docking technology, that should keep it on track.

THEY MADE INDIA'S SPACE PROGRAMME

Dr Vikram Sarabhai is considered the Father of the Indian Space Programme. The establishment of ISRO was one of his greatest achievements.

Dr K. Kasturirangan was the director of ISRO Satellite Centre (now URSC) from 1990 to 1994. In April 1994, he took over as chairman of ISRO. He laid the foundation for the *ASTROSAT* satellite project and conceptualised the Moon mission, *Chandrayaan-1*, and steered it to the stage of approval by the government.

Mr R. Aravamudan was the first of the engineers to join India's space programme in 1962. He became director of Thumba Equatorial Rocket Launching Station (TERLS) in the early 1970s and director of SDSC in 1989.

Prof. Satish Dhawan was the Indian rocket scientist who succeeded Dr Vikram Sarabhai as chairman of ISRO in 1972. After his death in 2002, the SHAR at Sriharikota, Andhra Pradesh was renamed the Satish Dhawan Space Centre in his honour.

Dr K. Radhakrishnan started his career as an avionics engineer in the Space Science and Technology Centre (now VSSC) in 1971. He was director, Vikram Sarabhai Space Centre, the lead centre for launch vehicle technology in ISRO, from 2007 to 2009. In 2009, he took over as chairman of ISRO and led it to achieve 37 space missions.

Prof. Yash Pal was an Indian scientist and educator who played a leading role in the application of space technology for mass communication and education. He was known especially for his contributions to the study of cosmic rays.

Dr A.P.J. Abdul Kalam was an aerospace scientist and a phenomenal teacher, who also served as the 11th President of India. He joined ISRO in 1969 as director of the *SLV-3* project, India's first indigenously designed and produced *SLV*.

Dr G. Madhavan Nair started his career at the TERLS in 1967. Since then, he has held various positions, rising to the position of director, VSSC, in 1999. He was one of the key persons of the pioneering *SLV-3* project team, in charge of the electronic integration and check-out of the vehicle.

Prof. U.R. Rao was a versatile space scientist and a technologist par excellence. He undertook the responsibility for the establishment of satellite technology in India in 1972. The ISRO Satellite Centre (ISAC) in Bengaluru has been renamed U.R. Rao Satellite Centre (URSC) in his honour.

A.S. Kiran Kumar is a highly accomplished space scientist and engineer. He began his career in ISRO by joining SAC in 1975. In March 2012, he took over as director of SAC. He was chairman of ISRO from January 2015 to January 2018.

Dr K. Sivan, the present chairman of ISRO, joined ISRO in 1982 in the *PSLV* project. He was the chief mission architect for the successful launch of 104 satellites in a single flight of *PSLV* in 2017.

SCIENTISTS OF INDIAN ORIGIN WHO CATALYSE NASA MISSIONS

Little known in their homeland, these brilliant individuals of Indian origin have played key roles in space-related discoveries and missions of NASA.

Kalpana Chawla emigrated to the US and became a naturalised citizen in the 1980s. She was selected as an astronaut candidate in 1994 and went for her first mission in 1997 on *Columbia STS-87*, becoming the first Indian woman to go to space.

Sunita Williams became a household name in India, being the second American female astronaut of Indian origin at NASA. She set the record for the longest cumulative spacewalk time by a female astronaut as well as the longest spaceflight by a woman.

Dr Ashwin Vasavada is the project scientist for the Mars Science Laboratory Rover (*Curiosity*) mission. He has also been a part of several spacecraft missions by NASA, such as the Galileo Mission to Jupiter, the Cassini Mission to Saturn, Mars Polar Lander and Mars Odyssey.

Dr Suresh B. Kulkarni has been recognised by NASA for 55 successful NASA rocket launches under the Space Shuttle Programme. Some notable shuttle missions that he was involved in include deployment of the *Magellan* spacecraft to Venus, the *Galileo* spacecraft to Jupiter, the Hubble Space Telescope and the Shuttle-Mir (the Russian space station) docking.

Born in Kolkata, Dr Amitabha Ghosh is a space scientist who works on Mars projects for NASA. He did his bachelor's and master's degrees in science from IIT Kharagpur. Currently, Ghosh serves as chair of the Science Operation Group for the Mars Exploration Rover Mission.

Dr Anita Sengupta is project manager at NASA Jet Propulsion Laboratory. She designed the 70-feet parachute that slowed the descent of the *Curiosity* rover onto Mars in March 2012. In 2016, she created a state of matter called the Bose-Einstein Condensate, as part of NASA's Cold Atom Laboratory, onboard the ISS.

One of the most celebrated scientists at NASA, Vadodara-born Dr Kamlesh Lulla is director of the University Research, Collaboration and Partnership Office at NASA's Johnson Space Centre in Houston.

Fondly known as Dr Lika, Dr Madhulika Guhathakurta is lead programme scientist for NASA's 'Living with a Star' programme, which focusses on understanding and predicting Sun's diverse effects on Earth, human technology and astronauts in space. She is most famous for leading the cause of heliophysics, the study of the Sun and its effect on the solar system.

Dr Sharmila Bhattacharya is director of research in the Biomodel Performance Laboratory of the Space Biosciences Division, NASA Ames Research Centre, California. As the director of research, she is responsible for overseeing that the research conducted is in accordance with NASA standards.

A nanotechnology expert, Dr Meyya Meyyappan is chief scientist for Exploration Technology at NASA Ames Research Centre, California. A highly decorated nanoscientist and an expert, Dr Meyyappan is known for his outstanding contribution to carbon nanotube application development.

CAREERS IN SPACE

India is one of the leading countries in space technology. There are several universities, research organisations and institutions that are actively involved in research and development in space science and technology. Kerala, in particular, is a major educational hub in this field, with the Indian Institute of Space Science and Technology (IIST), Thiruvananthapuram leading the way.

SPACE SCIENCE: A HIGHLY SPECIALISED CAREER IN INDIA

Initially, astronomy and astrophysics, planetary atmospheres, Earth sciences and solar system studies were broadly classified under astronomy. However, the recent interest in space has led to further categorisation of space science into numerous sub-branches—cosmology, stellar science, planetary science and astronomy—making 'space science and technology' a highly specialised career in India.

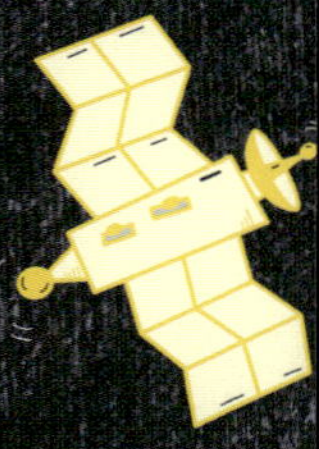

WHERE TO STUDY

IIST, Kerala, is a government-aided institute and deemed university for pursuing space science. It offers specialised courses in space science and technology. It functions as an autonomous body under the Department of Space, Government of India. It is the first university in Asia to be solely dedicated to the study and research on outer space. There are various undergraduate and postgraduate programmes to pick from, here. These include:

- Undergraduate: 4-Year B.Tech. (Aerospace Engineering); 4-Year B.Tech. (Electronics and Communication Engineering, Avionics)
- Dual Degree: 5-Year course comprising of B. Tech. (Engineering Physics); Master of Science/M. Tech. programme
- Postgraduate: M.Tech (Thermal and Propulsion; Aerodynamics and Flight Mechanics; Structures and Design; RF and Microwave Engineering; Digital Signal Processing; VLSI and Microsystems Control Systems; Power Electronics; Machine Learning and Computing; Materials Science and Technology; Optical Engineering; Solid State Technology; Earth System Science; Science Geoinformatics); Master of Science (Astronomy and Astrophysics)

These courses are open to students with requisite degrees, but a few seats are reserved for DoS and ISRO scientists and engineers. The academic programmes have been formulated to strengthen the fundamentals, experience the realities through practical work, and enhance knowledge and understanding in the areas relevant and related to space. Other colleges and institutes for study of space science and technology are Birla Institute of Technology, Mesra, Jharkhand; Aryabhatta Knowledge Institute of Science and Technology, Patna, Bihar; Sri Venkateshwara University, Tirupati, Andhra Pradesh.

QUALIFICATIONS REQUIRED

To make a career in space science, applications or technology, proficiency in physics, chemistry and mathematics is mandatory. The minimum educational qualification for joining a relevant bachelor's programme is 10+2 with physics, chemistry and mathematics.

Admission to IIST can be secured on the basis of ranks obtained in the Joint Entrance Examination conducted by IITs. All candidates who are placed in the extended list of IIT-JEE are eligible to apply in the first phase.

Students can also seek admission in a postgraduation course, in space science and technology and other space-related fields, after getting a three-year bachelor's degree in physics, chemistry or mathematics from any Indian university.

Undergraduate programmes at IIST offer liberal assistantships to meritorious students. So if a student can secure the stipulated minimum academic requirement, their education can be 'completely free'. This performance-based financial assistance provided by DoS gives ISRO and DoS the first right to absorb B. Tech. graduates of IIST into the vacancies notified by ISRO in that particular discipline and year.

CAREER PROSPECTS

A degree in space science and technology opens up employment opportunities for individuals. Depending on their qualifications and skills, they can explore job prospects in ISRO, Defence Research and Development Organisation (DRDO), Hindustan Aeronautics Limited (HAL), National Aeronautical Laboratories (NAL) and the aerospace industry in India.

Astronomers and astrophysicists can also seek opportunities in national observatories, space-research agencies, science museums and planetariums, and even designing and manufacturing telescopes, writing software and performing several tasks at ground-based observatories and space laboratories.

SPACE QUIZ

1. India's domestic communication system uses the *INSAT* and *GSAT* series of geostationary satellites. Which was the first Indian-built communications satellite?
(a) *Aryabhata*
(b) *APPLE*
(c) *INSAT-1A*
(d) *SROSS*

2. Today, India has state-of-the-art launch facilities for launching the most advanced geostationary satellites. Where was India's first rocket-launching facility located?
(a) Sriharikota
(b) Thumba
(c) Mahendragiri
(d) Chandipur

3. India has developed different launch vehicles for launching different satellites. Which of the following pairs is not matched correctly?
(a) *Rohini–SLV3*
(b) *IRS–PSLV*
(c) *INSAT–GSLV*
(d) *SROSS–PSLV*

4. Several of India's *INSAT*s have been launched from the launch centre of the European Space Agency at Kourou in French Guiana. Which was the first Indian satellite to be launched from Kourou?
(a) *INSAT-1B*
(b) *INSAT-2A*
(c) *APPLE*
(d) *IRS-1A*

5. Which was the first satellite launched by an Indian rocket?
(a) *Aryabhata*
(b) *Rohini*
(c) *IRS-1A*
(d) *SROSS*

6. As of 2019, who is the only Indian to have gone to space?
(a) Kalpana Chawla
(b) Rakesh Sharma
(c) Ravish Malhotra
(d) Ravish Sharma

7. The most powerful X-ray observatory placed in the Earth's orbit is named after an Indian astrophysicist. Who is he?
(a) Meghnad Saha
(b) Subrahmanyan Chandrasekhar
(c) Vikram Sarabhai
(d) M.K. Vainu Bappu

8. India's space centres are located in various places. Which of the following pairs is not matched correctly?
(a) SAC–Bengaluru
(b) VSSC–Thiruvananthapuram
(c) MCF–Hassan
(d) URSC–Bengaluru

9. Who was the first Chairman of ISRO?
(a) Prof. Satish Dhawan
(b) Prof. Yash Pal
(c) Prof. U.R. Rao
(d) Dr Vikram Sarabhai

10. Which of the following is not related to India's space programme?
(a) ISTRAC
(b) INCOSPAR
(c) URSC
(d) POTUS

11. Which of the following is not a multipurpose satellite?
(a) *INSAT-1B*
(b) *INSAT-2A*
(c) *INSAT-3B*
(d) *INSAT-4A*

12. Which of the following is India's first dedicated satellite for weather observation?
(a) *APPLE*
(b) *Kalpana-1*
(c) *Rohini*
(d) *INSAT-4A*

13. What is the largest number of satellites ever launched in a single flight of a rocket?
(a) 30
(b) 83
(c) 104
(d) 106

14. Which of the following is not a remote-sensing satellite?
(a) *RESOURCESAT*
(b) *OCEANSAT*
(c) *CARTOSAT*
(d) *ASTROSAT*

15. How many satellites are used for India's NavIC system?
(a) 5
(b) 7
(c) 24
(d) 31

16. Which of the following is not a satellite navigation system?
(a) GLONASS
(b) GPS
(c) NavIC
(d) SROSS

17. When was the first countrywide television broadcast experiment (SITE) conducted in India?
(a) 1972–73
(b) 1975–76
(c) 1977–79
(d) 1980–81

18. Which of the following centres of ISRO is responsible for the design and fabrication of launch vehicles?
(a) VSSC
(b) URSC
(c) SDSC
(d) NRSC

19. Which of the following satellites can sense or 'observe' the Earth using radar beams from space, day and night?
(a) *EMISAT*
(b) *RISAT*
(c) *HysIS*
(d) *NovaSAR*

20. Nano satellites are very small satellites. How much do they weigh?
(a) Less than 0.5 kg
(b) Less than 1 kg
(c) Less than 5 kg
(d) Less than 10 kg

ANSWERS

1. (b) *APPLE*
2. (b) Thumba
3. (b) *SROSS-PSLV*
4. (c) *APPLE*
5. (b) *Rohini*
6. (b) Rakesh Sharma
7. (b) Subrahmanyan Chandrasekhar
8. (a) SAC–Bengaluru
9. (d) Dr Vikram Sarabhai
10. (d) POTUS
11. (c) *INSAT-3B*
12. (b) *Kalpana-1*
13. (c) 104
14. (d) *ASTROSAT*
15. (b) 7
16. (d) SROSS
17. (b) 1975–76
18. (a) VSSC
19. (b) *RISAT*
20. (d) Less than 10 kg

GLOSSARY

Apogee: The point closest to the Earth in the orbit of a satellite

Asteroids: Rocky objects that orbit the Sun between Mars and Jupiter

Astronaut: A person trained to travel and work in space

Booster: Solid rocket boosters operate in parallel with the main rocket engines for the first two minutes of flight, to provide additional thrust to escape the gravitational pull of the Earth.

Chromosphere: The second of the three main layers in the Sun's atmosphere, roughly 3,000–5,000 km deep

Corona: The outermost part of the Sun's atmosphere that extends millions of kilometres into outer space

Crew module: A system in which astronauts stay when they go to space

Cryogenic engine: A rocket engine that uses liquid hydrogen and liquid oxygen as propellants

DTH: DTH stands for 'direct-to-home' television or radio, which is received directly from a satellite, without the intervention of a cable operator.

Geostationary orbit: A circular orbit 35,786 km above the Earth's equator, in which a satellite moving in the direction of the Earth's rotation appears stationary from the ground

GPS: Global Positioning System

GSLV: Geostationary Satellite Launch Vehicle

IDSN: Indian Deep Space Network

IRNSS: Indian Regional Navigation Satellite System

Lagrangian point: A location in space where the gravitational forces of two large bodies, such as the Earth and the Sun or the Earth and the Moon, balance out

Lander: A spacecraft that descends towards and comes to rest on the surface of an astronomical body

Launch window: A term used to describe a time period within which a particular space mission must be launched to reach its intended target

Launching pad: The surface from which a rocket is launched, typically consisting of a platform with a supporting structure

Methane: A colourless, odourless flammable gas, which is produced by certain living organisms, and is the main constituent of natural gas

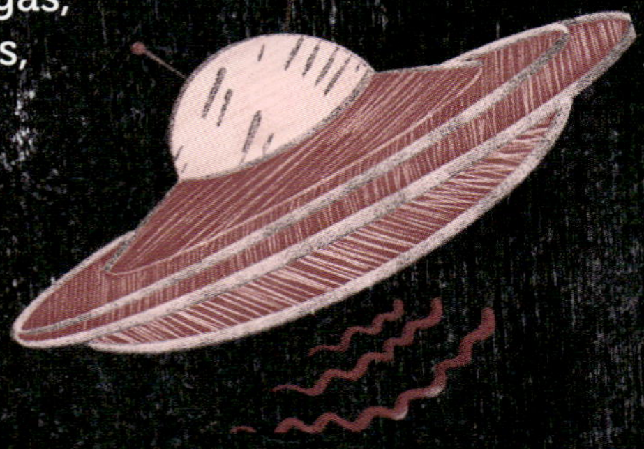

Methanogens: Methane-producing bacteria

NavIC: Navigation using Indian Constellation

Orbit raising: The process of gradually increasing the farthest point in the orbit of an Earth-orbiting satellite, using onboard rockets and the Earth's gravity

Orbiter: A space probe that orbits a planet or another astronomical object

Pad abort: A launch escape system where the crew module is separated and ejected to safety from the launch vehicle by small rockets

Payload: For a rocket, the payload can be a satellite, space probe, or spacecraft carrying humans, animals or cargo

Perigee: The point in the orbit of the Moon or a satellite at which it is nearest to the Earth

Photosphere: The lowest layer of the Sun's atmosphere

Polar orbit: An orbit in which a satellite passes above or nearly above both poles of the body being orbited, such as the Earth or the Moon

PSLV: Polar Satellite Launch Vehicle

Remote sensing: The imaging of the Earth by a satellite or a high-flying aircraft to obtain information about it

Rocket stage: A part of a satellite-launching rocket; several stages mounted one above another fall away, beginning with the bottom-most, as the rocket rises

Rover: A space exploration vehicle designed to move across the surface of a planet or other celestial bodies

SAR: Synthetic Aperture Radar

SITE: Satellite Instructional Television Experiment

Solid-propellant rocket: Rockets that use solid propellants

Sounding rocket: An instrument-carrying rocket designed to take measurements and perform scientific experiments during its flight

Space shuttle: A partially reusable low-Earth orbital spacecraft system that was operated from 1981 to 2011 by NASA

STEP: Satellite Telecommunication Experimental Project

Transponder: A device on satellites for receiving a radio signal and automatically transmitting it at a different frequency

VSAT: Very Small Aperture Terminal

Weightlessness: The absence of the sensation of weight while in space

ABOUT THE AUTHOR

Indian science editor and writer Biman Basu has been deeply committed to popularising science through print and electronic media since 1967. He was the editor of the monthly *Science Reporter* for 30 years. He has authored more than 45 books and scripted several radio serials on science. Basu is the winner of the 1994 NCSTC National Award for best science and technology coverage in the mass media and Kishore Jnan-Bijnan prize, 1990, for popular science writing in Bengali. He is a member of the Indian Science Writers' Association (life, secretary 1988–92), Indian Science Congress Association (life), National Geographic Society and Planetary Society.

CREDITS

A big thanks to ISRO and NASA for the permission to use photographs and information available on their website.

6–7: Artist Illustration; NASA
8–9: NASA
10–11: NASA
12–13: NASA; ISRO
14–15: NASA
16–17: NASA
22–23: NASA; ISRO
24–25: ISRO
26–27: ISRO
28–29: ISRO; NASA
30–31: ISRO
32–33: ISRO; NASA
34–35: ISRO; NASA
36–37: ISRO; NASA
38–39: ISRO; NASA
40–41: ISRO; NASA
42–43: NASA
44–45: Artist Illustration by Mistunee Chowdhury; NASA
46–47: ISRO; NASA
48–49: NASA
50–51: ISRO; NASA
52–53: ISRO; NASA
54–55: Artist Illustration by Kevin Gill (United States); Mistunee Chowdhury; NASA
56–57: ISRO; NASA
58–59: Artist Illustration by Mistunee Chowdhury; NASA
60–61: ISRO; NASA; Pixabay
62–63: ISRO; NASA
64–65: ISRO; NASA
66–67: ISRO; NASA
68–69: Artist Illustration by Mistunee Chowdhury
70–71: Artist Illustration by Mistunee Chowdhury
72–73: Artist Illustration by Ateendriya; NASA
74–75: Artist Illustration by Ateendriya
76–77: Artist Illustration by Ateendriya
78–79: Artist Illustration by Ateendriya